THE OUR FATHER

FR KEN BARKER MGL

Published in 2021 by Connor Court Publishing Pty Ltd

Copyright © Ken Barker

All rights reserved. No part of this book may be reproduced or transmitted in any form or by any means, electronic or mechanical, including photocopying, recording or by any information storage and retrieval system, without prior permission in writing from the publisher.

Connor Court Publishing Pty Ltd
PO Box 7257
Redland Bay QLD 4165
sales@connorcourt.com
www.connorcourtpublishing.com.au
Phone 0497 900 685

ISBN: 9781922449634

Front Cover Design: Lawence Yuen

Printed in Australia

The Our Father

FR KEN BARKER MGL

Connor Court Publishing

Nihil Obstat:

Fr Trenton van Reesch STL   Censor Deputatis

Imprimatur:

Most Rev Christopher Prowse DD STD

Archbishop Canberra and Goulburn

Acknowledgments

I wish to thank Selina Hasham for her careful examination of the text, and to Lawence Yuen for the cover design. Also I am grateful to the MGL brothers who graciously allowed me the space to complete the manuscript.

Bible Quotations are taken from the Jerusalem Bible

CONTENTS

Foreword   7

Introduction   9

1) *Our Father who art in Heaven*   17

2) *Hallowed be they name*   33

3) *Thy kingdom come*   49

4) *Thy will be done on earth as it is in Heaven*   69

5) *Give us this day our daily bread*   95

6) *Forgive us our trespasses as we forgive those who trespass against us*   109

7) *Lead us not into temptation*   125

8) *Deliver us from evil*   135

Endnotes   147

Our Father, who art in heaven,

hallowed be thy name;

thy kingdom come,

thy will be done

on earth as it is in heaven.

Give us this day our daily bread,

and forgive us our trespasses,

as we forgive those who trespass against us;

and lead us not into temptation,

but deliver us from evil

FOREWORD

Sin is like a stroke. People who have suffered a stroke have to re-learn the most basic and natural skills, like speech. So too, because of sin, we have to learn the most basic and natural skill that we call prayer. Prayer is native to the human being; we're made for it. But after the Fall we need to re-learn the language of Paradise which is our true home. We need to re-learn our mother-tongue. That's why the disciples ask Jesus to teach them to pray; and it's why Jesus teaches them, and us, the unforgettable words of the Our Father, which have never fallen silent since the time of his teaching.

The words are simple because Jesus doesn't want his disciples to babble as the pagans do. But the words are also infinite, because they take us into the inner life of God where the Son speaks to the Father. That's why interpretation of the Lord's Prayer can never end; the words never cease to yield fresh meaning; they are old but eternally new.

In these pages, Fr Ken Barker explores Jesus' teaching on prayer; and in doing so, he teaches us what it is to pray at this time when prayer is more important than ever. Fr Ken teaches us afresh what it is to listen to Jesus, to learn from him and to enter with him into the heart of God, becoming daughters and sons of the Father, sisters and brothers to each other.

Archbishop Mark Coleridge, Brisbane

INTRODUCTION

Teach us to Pray

When the Church teaches us to pray she gives us the "Our Father". Why? Because this is how Jesus taught his apostles to pray. One day, when they had been watching Jesus rapt in silent prayer, the apostles asked him, "Lord, teach us to pray!" (Lk 11:1) They wanted what they could see in him. They were inspired by the deep communion he had with the Father. It was visible in his countenance, his whole disposition, as he prayed. Have you ever had the privilege of observing a holy person rapt in prayer? It is so attractive to one's spirit, to the deepest longing in the human heart. The disciples were drawn by grace as they became fascinated by Jesus' prayer. His communion with the Father was irresistible. His interior consolation from the Father's presence was so visually appealing that the apostles were eager to share his experience.

In the apostles' request we can also possibly detect echoes of frustration. Maybe they had struggled to pray and found it less than satisfying; even quite alienating. Maybe they envied what they saw in Jesus – his joy and peace as he communed with the Father, his capacity to take any trial or difficulty into prayer and come out refreshed and renewed; how he would often turn to prayer when seeking the way ahead and gain clarity and assurance of the next step to take. They couldn't help but notice how many times he withdrew from their company to go into the hills or to some other remote place where he could be alone to seek the Father's heart. This was no doubt a growing mystery to them. What was his secret? They figured it was prayer, but maybe a new way of praying they had not observed in the Scribes and Pharisees.

There was something radically different about the way Jesus prayed. All of this was behind the simple plea, "teach us to pray". Surely we too need to beg the Lord for this gift as well! Only the Lord can teach us to pray. Yes, there are good spiritual directors who can give us pointers and techniques to open ourselves in the presence of God; but nothing is more effective than simply begging the Lord himself, even if it comes out of frustration and irritation at the poverty of our experience of prayer: "Lord, teach me to pray!"

Jesus' Answer

Jesus' answer to the apostles was to give them what we now know as the "Our Father". Ironically, what was never intended to be a formal prayer rattled off by rote, has become just that. In Matthew's account Jesus prefaces the gift by warning "In your prayers do not babble as the pagans, for they think that by using many words they will make themselves heard". Unfortunately, what Jesus warned about "the pagans" may be found in Christians praying today. The many "Our Fathers" and "Hail Marys" we rattle off can be mindless repetition with little depth of communion.

What is now stylised as the "Our Father" is indeed one of the Church's greatest treasures. We pray it every day at Mass, during the Liturgy of the Hours, and in the liturgy of most of the sacraments. It is the Lord's own prayer. We cannot improve on it. Yet, it is not meant to remain a formula that we use much like a Christian anthem. We need to plumb the depths of its meaning. It is the paradigm of prayer. To really know the "Our Father" is to discover all we need to know about prayer. As this revelation dawns we will surely begin to utter the words in a new and vigorous way, not by rote but with the sincere intention of the heart.

I think of the many times throughout my life when I have said the "Our Father". How many times have I really prayed it? Sadly, not enough times. Yet this prayer is potential dynamite for the soul, able to burst open the heart, expressing our deepest desires and expectations of God's action in the soul. This is the prayer of Jesus himself; the incarnate Son of God who knows the deepest needs of his human brothers and sisters. He gives us the words addressed to the Father uttered from his own heart.

Praying from the Heart

Usually when we engage in communication with others the words come from a thought, an emotion or an image that has been born in the mind and then articulated. We speak spontaneously from what is within us. It is good to do the same as we speak to God. The Spirit stirs the heart and we express our needs, our joys, our suffering, our sorrow for sin, gratitude for God's many gifts. This intensely personal way of praying is paramount in the spiritual tradition. We are encouraged by the saints to fall more in love with the Lord and open our hearts spontaneously to him.

However, there will always be a place for prayer formulas taken from Scripture or provided for us by holy men and women, or given in the Church's liturgical prayer. In this case the dynamic is different. We are voicing prayer formulated by another. The heart needs to own this prayer, otherwise the exercise is empty. For instance, when we pray a psalm we are using someone else's prayer which originally had depth of experiential meaning for the psalmist. We trust the Spirit will draw us into the experience which birthed the psalm. It is a similar dynamic when praying the "Our Father". The more we can appreciate the significance of the words the more we can pray from the heart. In this case, it is Jesus who has directly given us the words. To pray these words can evoke in us the experience of Jesus himself and all the significance that these words had for him. We come to know the Lord's heart more, and can be more readily formed in his ways.

When we pray the Our Father we are joining in the prayer of Jesus. We pray the seven petitions confidently in the name of Jesus and benefit from all the promises Jesus gave to his disciples: "the Father will give you anything you ask in my name" (Jn 15:16), and "I tell you solemnly, anything you ask for from the Father he will grant in my name" (Jn 16:23). When prayed from the heart, in union with Jesus, we can be sure our prayer is answered. Praying to the Father, in the name of Jesus, by the Holy Spirit is the core of Christian prayer.

Structure of the Lord's Prayer

The prayer opens with an initial address to God as Father in heaven. This beginning remains the pivotal foundation throughout the whole prayer. Undoubtedly everything falls into place for us when we are able to genuinely turn to God, as our Father; we know who we are as sons and daughters of God in *the* Son of God, through the inspiration of the Holy Spirit.

After calling upon the Father, we address seven petitions to him. The first three are "thou petitions", which concern God himself and his action in the world. The other four are "we petitions", and are concerned with our hopes, needs and relationships. This structure has a similarity to the Ten Commandments, which begin with three commandments on loving God and then seven on loving our neighbour. In both cases we are first acknowledging the primacy of

God in our lives and everything we do. Then as a result of our love for God we express our desire for right living and ordered relationships. To approach God, we need first to step aside from ourselves and open up to God himself. We become truly human by first turning to God with all our heart, soul, mind and strength. Then in communion with him we come to know what he wants of us, and are inspired to ask for our deepest needs.

Teaching on Prayer

In this book I intend to explain as best I can the meaning of each phrase in the Our Father and hence help the reader to appreciate its significance for his or her personal prayer. Before doing this I want to demonstrate the basic movement towards deeper encounter with the Lord which is implied in the flow of Jesus' prayer. I am drawing upon Teresa of Avila's teaching given in her so-called "catechism on prayer", her classic work entitled *The Way of Perfection*.[1]

Teresa testifies that a number of her sisters who were quite simple and docile to the Holy Spirit would often be lifted into intense union with God through praying the Lord's prayer. Hence she highly values vocal prayer. She teaches that this prayer form can be the vehicle the Lord uses to take us fully into his heart of love for the Father, and hence into surrender of one's being to the Father and his will for us.

So at the outset I want to give a summary of how Teresa shows the Our Father contains within it the way towards contemplative prayer. Firstly, the Lord gives us the enormous gift of calling God, Father. This revelation of itself is enough to have us moved into ecstasy. If we really knew what it meant to call God, Father, we would be immediately caught up in such intense love that we could go no further. We would be overcome by who we are addressing and who we are as his sons and daughters. Nothing more would matter. As Teresa says, "Does it seem right to you now that even though we recite these first words vocally we should fail to let our intellects understand and our hearts break in pieces at seeing such love".[2]

Reflecting on the words "who art in heaven" Teresa speaks of the prayer of recollection, or the prayer of companionship. For Teresa, prayer is going aside with your best friend and having conversation with him. She points out, "God is everywhere...in summary, wherever God is there is heaven"[3]. Heaven is being in the presence of God. Heaven is within us. Teresa unforgettably refers to "this little heaven of our soul, where the Maker of heaven and earth is present".[4] She calls this grace-filled discovery the prayer of "recollection"; because "the soul collects its faculties together and enters within itself to be with its God".[5] This breakthrough to genuine interiority is necessary for all who are desiring deeper union with God. We recall the prayer of St Augustine who, after his conversion, lamented to God, "Late have I loved you O Beauty so ancient and so new. Late have I loved you. You were within me, and I was outside; and I fell on the good things of your creation"[6] as if that would satisfy. Only when he was overwhelmed by the grace of God did Augustine realise God was already within him waiting for life-changing encounter.

In this prayer of recollection the fire of God's love burns within the soul. If the fire starts to die down, then a few thoughts or a single scriptural word is enough to enflame the fire again. Because we are near to the source, it takes little effort to stoke the fire again and keep the soul in heartfelt love for our closest Friend. Teresa urges her sisters:

> Out of love for the Lord, get used to praying the Our Father with this recollection, and you will see the benefit before long. This is a manner of praying that the soul gets so quickly

used to that it doesn't go astray, nor do the faculties become restless, as time will tell. I only ask that you try this method, even though it may mean some struggle; everything involves struggle before the habit is acquired.[7]

Contemplative Experience

To teach about the onset of contemplation as such, which Teresa calls the "prayer of quiet", she comments on the petitions "hallowed by thy name" and "thy kingdom come". This "prayer of quiet" cannot be obtained by our own efforts but is a sheer supernatural gift from God. However, we can dispose ourselves for the gift. The Lord hears our petition and we are able to truly praise and "hallow" his name.[8] In order to enable us to hallow his name the Lord gives us his kingdom here on earth. We experience a foretaste of his kingdom to come. We receive the interior blessing of contemplation.

In this "prayer of quiet" the faculties of intellect, will, memory and imagination are stilled. However, only the will is totally captive to the love of God. The person is simply caught up in what Jesus declared as "the one thing necessary". You will remember the scene in the gospel when Martha was complaining about Mary sitting at the feet of Jesus, absorbing his presence, while she was working hard in the kitchen. He replied "Martha, Martha, you worry and fret about so many things, but only one is really necessary, Mary has chosen the better part" (Lk 10:42). In this mode of quiet prayer the intellect and the imagination may roam out of control but the will is completely captured by the love of the Lord. Teresa describes it thus:

> Persons in this prayer see that only this one thing is necessary, and everything else disturbs them. They don't want the body to move because it seems they would thereby lose that

peace; thus they don't dare stir. It pains them to speak; in their saying 'Our Father' just once a whole hour passes. They are so close that they see they are understanding as though through signs.[9]

Teresa then connects the next petition, "thy will be done on earth as it is in heaven", to what has gone before. Now that the grace has been given through contemplation we are able to respond to the Lord's goodness by giving over our wills to him in return for his love. Only after we have received the wonderful gift of contemplative love is it possible for us to do his will in all circumstances and surrender to his will when unexpected calamities come our way.[10] We become unstoppable in our commitment to Jesus and filled with fervour for his kingdom.

The Our Father, then, has potential to lead us into the highest levels of prayer. When we pray it in the Spirit and yield our hearts to God we can be drawn into the very heart of Jesus for the Father. We can exclaim in and through Jesus "my food is to do the will of the One who sent me". The apostles never forgot this prayer, and it has been faithfully passed down through the centuries. It is the greatest prayer bar none. It contains the entire content of the gospel, the fullness of Christian prayer, and the paradigm of the Christian way of life, all in the *ipsissima verba* of Jesus himself (i.e. his very own words). Consequently, I will now proceed in an attempt to dissect each phrase of the prayer, seeking to expound its meaning and show how it takes us into communion with God.

OUR FATHER, WHO ART IN HEAVEN

"Abba", Father

The secret of Jesus which he came to share with us is his unique relationship with the Father. "No one has ever seen God; it is only the Son, who is nearest to the Father's heart, who has made him known" (Jn 1:18). From all eternity the Son has been turned towards the Father in a mutual exchange of love. Now in time the Son has become one of us, and he wants to draw us into this unique relationship. Jesus' prayer is a vehicle for this encounter. At the Last Supper Jesus encouraged his disciples not to be afraid because he was leaving them. He was returning to the Father to prepare a place for them in his heart. He assured them "there are many rooms in my Father's house". He added, "If you know me you know my Father too".

Phillip was not satisfied with this mysterious language. He pleaded with Jesus to just show them the Father; then they would be satisfied. Jesus was exasperated, "Have I been with you all this time, Phillip, and you still do not know me? To have seen me is to have seen the Father" (Jn 14:7-9). That's the whole point of Jesus' mission; to reveal the heart of the Father to us; to bring us into the same intimacy he has with the Father. Only through Jesus do we come to know what the Father is like.

The Aramaic word for Father that the gospel writers record from Jesus' own lips is *Abba*. Much has been written about this. While there are different shades of interpretation of the term, every scholar agrees that it is a term of affection and endearment, indicating close familiarity and intimacy. While it has some foreshadowing in the Old

Testament notion of Father, scholars agree that Jesus' use of *Abba* is radically unique. In the mother tongue of Jesus children customarily addressed their earthly father as *Abba*. But the Jewish religious tradition did not favour such a term of intimacy when speaking to God. The word "Father" used in the Old Testament does not connote this close personal, affectionate embrace.

Abba, on the lips of Jesus, speaks of the dependent attitude of children who totally trust their Father for everything. This is how Jesus speaks of the Father in his teachings. He tells us not to worry about the basics of food, clothing, and provision: "Your Father well knows you need them" (Lk 12:30). He also reminds us that fathers do not give their children a stone when they ask for bread, or a snake instead of a fish, or a scorpion if they asked for an egg. He then continues, "If you then who are evil know how to give good gifts to your children, how much more will your Father give good things to those who ask him" (Mt 7:9ff). That's what we expect when we pray the Our Father. In Luke's version Jesus says "how much more will the heavenly Father give you *the Holy Spirit* if you ask him" (Lk 11:13). This is even more profound. God's purpose is to give his very self to us as we trust him with our lives.

Beloved Sons and Daughters

When Jesus rose up out of the waters of the Jordan after being baptised by John, the Spirit descended upon him and he heard the words, "You are my Son, the Beloved, my favour rests on you" (Lk 3:22). As a young man about to move into mission Jesus was confirmed in who he is in relation to the Father. He knew himself as Son. This was his deepest secret; the assurance of the Father's unconditional and constant love. In his humanity this made all the difference. No doubt he often heard those words echoing in his heart; words repeated in the experience on the Mount of Transfiguration just before he decisively moved towards his passion. This utmost confidence in his Father carried him forward. Often going aside to lonely places to commune with the Father, he always found the inner human resource to embrace whatever suffering was before him. Unconditional trust in the Father was the secret of his perseverance in the Father's will unto the end.

In our baptism we were begotten as sons and daughters of the Father by the action of the Holy Spirit. St Paul was well aware of the critical importance of knowing *Abba,* Father: "Everyone moved by the Spirit is a son of God. The spirit you received is not the spirit of slaves bringing fear into your lives again; it is the spirit of sons, and it makes us cry out, '*Abba,* Father'" (Rom 8:14-15). Every baptised person ought to hear echoing in his or her heart the same words that Jesus heard, "you are my son (daughter), my beloved, my favour rests on you". This means we walk with a new assurance and confidence, trusting in our Father God for everything. There's no longer any fear of being diminished in the eyes of others, or feeling we don't match up to others' expectations, or left in a mess of disappointment when failure comes, or succumbing to distress when others speak disparagingly about us.

Foundation of our Identity

Our identity is not founded in our performance or in what others think of us, but in who I am as a son or a daughter of God. In Galatians Paul assures us that we no longer have to be slaves to bad habits or sinful ways, nor captive to social stereotypes or religious legalities. We have been set free by Christ. We have been redeemed and have become adopted sons and daughters: "The proof that you are sons (daughters) is that God has sent the Spirit of his Son into our hearts: the Spirit that cries *'Abba*, Father', and it is this that makes you a son (daughter); you are not a slave anymore. And if God has made you son (daughter), then he has made you heir" (Gal 4:6-7).

To know Jesus is to know our place in the Father's embrace. Jesus said to his apostles, "I do not call you servants anymore since a servant does not know his master's business. I call you friends" (Jn 15:15). And what is the sign of this friendship? Why does he call us his friend? "because I have revealed to you all that I know of my Father's heart". This is what the Lord's prayer is about. Through our friendship with Jesus we come into the revelation of the Father's heart. Prayer is firstly about God's action in us rather than our aspiration towards him. We cry *"Abba"* because we are in and with Jesus, and we find ourselves captured by the Father's immense and unconditional love for us. The more we cry *"Abba"* the more the Father embraces us in tender love and mercy. Jesus opens up for us the way to the Father's heart. Nothing is more satisfying for the human soul; nothing more ennobling, nothing more elevating. In crying out *"Abba"* we are where we are meant to be, secure in his loving arms, no matter how the storm may rage around us, or how precarious our situation may be.

An image may help. I heard of a tight-rope walker in New York. He had set up a rope between two high buildings. As he walked the tight-rope a crowd gathered below. Then returning to the window of one of the buildings the stunt man did something incredibly irresponsible. He picked up his young son and carried him in his arms as he walked between the two buildings. The people below were aghast. When the man and his son came down safely the reporters interviewed them. They asked the little boy, "Weren't you afraid up there?" He answered, "No, I wasn't afraid. I was in my Daddy's arms!" This is the way we are to move through life; as sons and daughters of God. When we know this truth nothing troubles us no matter how calamitous it may seem, because "I am in my Daddy's arms".

Dare to Call Him Father

In the Roman liturgy when the priest invites us to pray the Our Father he says, "At the Saviour's command and formed by divine teaching, we *dare to say*". This reminds me of a book written by Bilquis Shiek some years ago entitled, *I Dared to Call Him Father*.[11] Bilquis was a highly-born Pakistani woman who had grown up as a Muslim but was searching within herself for answers. She had some dreams in which she identified figures such as John the Baptist, and even Christ. Somewhat disturbed she asked one of her Christian servants for a bible. She began to read secretly this forbidden text. Soon afterwards, one of her servants became sick and Bilquis took her to a hospital run by Catholic nuns. One day she was sitting by the bedside of the patient reading the bible when one of the nuns noticed. The Sister exclaimed with astonishment, "Why, Bilquis, you are reading the bible!" Bilquis replied, "Yes, I want to get to know your God. How can I get to know him?" The Sister must have had a moment of divine inspiration, because she gave Bilquis the advice she needed, "That's easy, when you go home just imagine yourself as a child on your father's knees and speak to him as papa". Bilquis took the advice. When she imagined herself in this place of intimacy and began to call God "papa" she was filled with a warmth all over her body. She was wrapped into an experience of his love which she never knew existed. Until then she only knew the almighty Allah, the ruler and king, who has beneficence and must be worshipped, but is too great to draw anyone into personal intimacy. She dared to call God, *Abba*. But, unfortunately, her newly found faith put her life in danger. She had to leave her homeland and she spent the rest of her life travelling the globe preaching of the Father's love.

Only by the Spirit's work within us can we have the courage to call God, *Abba*. In the Old Testament this way of praying was unknown. God was the great and mighty king of all, the Lord of heaven and earth, who gave his law to Moses on the mountain surrounded by fear and trembling. He was sometimes called Almighty Father, as the God who freely chose his people, delivered them from Egypt and steadfastly cherished them. But no one dared to pray to him as "Abba". The divine name was so holy that it could not be pronounced. When Moses asks God for his name he receives the revelation, YHWH ("I am who I am"). This name is mysterious, just as God is mysterious. It is both the revelation of a name and also the refusal to be named. It expresses God who is infinitely above everything that we can understand or say. He is hidden and beyond knowledge. We cannot express his name. Yet he is God who is close to humanity, especially to his chosen people. He is "God of Abraham, Isaac, and Jacob", who is caring for and liberating his people.

This Old Testament experience of God awaited the incarnation, when Jesus, the Son of God, could reveal the Father as *Abba*. Jesus himself is the way to the Father; only by his Spirit can we dare to pray "*Abba*, Father". The Holy Spirit now gives us a boldness not possible for the people of old. Now through the blood of Jesus we have "a right to enter the sanctuary" (Heb 19:19). We now have the gift of *parresia*, boldness in knowing the place that has been won for us by Jesus, and can pray with utmost confidence to our *Abba*, Father. "Let us be confident, then, in approaching the throne of grace, that we shall have mercy from him and find grace when we are in need of help" (Heb 4:16).

Healing the "Father Wound"

To be able to pray the Our Father from the heart we need to work on our operative image of God. By "operative" I mean the way we instinctively experience the notion of "father" in our hearts. We all know intellectually that God is our loving Father, but due to wounds of the past we can find it difficult to really experience him that way. We may need healing so we can genuinely experience ourselves as sons and daughters of a loving Father God. The way we experienced our earthly biological fathers or other father figures in our early years of life can shape the way we see God.

Some years ago a study done by Steve Biddulph of the way Australian men experience their fathers identified a number of negative images.[12] Some remembered their father as a tyrant around the house, a threatening and dominating figure. I remember one man who came to us for healing prayer who was having trouble because he was bursting out in anger within the family and putting his fist through walls. After some gentle probing it became evident that he had issues with his father. He recalled that as children, when they heard their father's footsteps on the gravel outside returning home from work, they would all freeze; another night of terror and uncertainty about what would happen. The healing prayer helped him to own the pain, forgive his father, and receive the touch of Jesus which enabled him not only to be a peaceful man about the house, but also to discover God as *Abba*.

In this survey other men experienced their father as being critical, rarely affirming them for anything good they had done, but negative and judgemental. If this was the dominant experience of our fathering, then we could easily project that image onto God as Father. Some men experienced their father as a "couch potato", lazing around the house, plonked in front of the TV with a tinnie, disengaged and relinquishing responsibility for important family matters. With that sort of fathering it is more than likely we would find it difficult to experience God as personally caring and willing to take our burdens and be genuinely present to us in our needs. A large group in the survey experienced their father as absent, too busy with his profession and associated activities or away from the home with mates pursuing his own pleasures. Again, the wound of the "absent father" can be so deep in us that we find it difficult to image God as close, intimate, and caring. How are we to experience the "tenderness of the heart of our God who visits us like the dawn from on high?" (Lk 1:78) Our earthly experience of "father" can be an unconscious barrier to us being able to genuinely pray to *Abba,* God.

Story of Healing

Praise be to God that healing can happen. Jesus wants to heal our hearts so we can open up to the experience of his Father, and share in this experience. My own father died when I was 21 years old. As he was severely jaundiced and slipping away from the debilitating effects of pancreatic cancer I held his hand in the hospital. But it was too late to say what needed to be said. I took the squeeze of his hand to mean he loved me. At the funeral as we carried out the coffin I wept profusely for the loss of my Dad, but my tears were also for what was unfinished in our relationship. Now it was too late. As with most people I simply buried the pain. But after receiving the new outpouring of the Holy Spirit many years later the painful memories began to surface. Jesus was beginning the healing process. I remembered how my Dad used to mock me and humiliate me before others, how he seemed to prefer my brothers over me, and how sometimes he had administered what was experienced by me as unjust punishment. As I owned the pain of these memories I was able to forgive him and invite Jesus into the wound to bring healing.

In a wonderful way Jesus then opened up to me the love of *Abba*, Father. I prayed Psalm 40 in a whole new way: "I waited, I waited for the Lord and he stooped down to me; he heard my cry. He lifted me up from the deadly pit, from the miry clay. He set my feet upon a rock and made my footsteps firm. He put a new song into my mouth, a song of praise to my God" (Ps 40:2-3). I experienced the Father lifting me up to himself and filling me with a new song of praise. This experience of being "lifted up" in his loving arms ministered to me deeply. Another text that spoke to me was from Hosea. The image is given of God reaching down to Israel as a father reaches down to lift up a child against his cheek. God says, "I was like someone who lifts an infant close against his cheek; stooping down to him I gave him his food" (Hos 11:4). This is what I was experiencing in prayer, held close to the Father's heart, secure in his arms, affirmed as his son and assured that I was unconditionally loved. I believe Jesus wants to heal all our hearts so we can be brought more deeply into the loving embrace of our *Abba*, Father.

To honour my father I must share the sequel to this story. At the beginning of 1999, which was proclaimed by Pope John Paul II as the "year of the Father", I was back at the family home in a country town in New South Wales. For seemingly no reason I was prompted to visit my father's grave in the cemetery at the edge of town. Standing at the foot of the grave I began to pray. Then I began weeping. A lost memory had surfaced. At the end of my final year at a boarding college I came back to the family home. My Dad told me with some excitement he had something to show me. He took me out to the back shed which was usually empty. Now it was occupied by an EH Holden car, the first car he had been able to purchase. Why? Because he had spent all his money making sure we were fed, clothed, and received the best education available. My tears were of gratitude for such a wonderfully provident father who gave everything for his children, and then died early at the age of 53 years. Now, my healing was complete, since any warping of my view of my father had been healed. Now the term "father" evokes in me an awareness of faithfulness, self-sacrificing love, dedication, affirmation, intimacy and affection.

Unconditional Love

Praying the Our Father is an expression of total trust in *Abba* whose love is not dependent on our performance. The cut-throat culture of the world tells us implicitly "I will love you *if* you are good looking, get good grades, make lots of money, or become famous"; or "I love you *but* that could change when adverse circumstances come upon us, or you get sick, or I just get sick of you". Having experienced conditional love from others it is hard for us to really believe anyone could love us without "ifs" or "buts". Jesus came to reveal to us God as *Abba*, Father, who will never abandon us, nor give up on us no matter what happens and regardless of how badly we perform. St Paul expressed it so beautifully when he said:

> For I am certain of this: neither death nor life, no angel, no prince, nothing that exists, nothing still to come, not any power, or height or depth, nor any created thing, can come between us and the love of God made visible in Christ Jesus our Lord (Rom 8: 38-39).

When we pray the Lord's Prayer we are claiming the truth that we are the beloved sons and daughters of God. This is our baptismal identity which cannot be stolen from us. I know who I am in Christ – a child of God. No pressure to perform or to be a success will govern me, even when it comes to the pursuit of holiness. I will not fall into the perfectionist trap; feeling my worth and value is dependent upon my performance and how others see me. I will know myself as a beloved son or daughter of God. I will rest secure in his gaze upon me. Jesus teaches me the secret of his heart, the inner knowledge of the Father's love, which carried him through the darkness of his Passion. In his humanity Jesus never forgot the words of the Father, whispering in his heart, "You are my Son, the Beloved, my favour rests on you". As we pray the Lord's Prayer we also hear that whisper of the Father in the depths of our soul, "You are my son, my daughter, my beloved, my blessing is upon you".

"Our" Father

So far I have been emphasising the personal intimacy which we experience by addressing God as *"Abba"*. But the prayer Jesus gave us is uttered in the first person plural. We speak to God as "our" Father, and the last four petitions are entreating the Father for "us". This tells us something important. As Pope Benedict says, "in the act of prayer the totally personal and communal must always pervade each other". He goes on to say, "The 'we' of the praying community and the utterly personal intimacy that can be shared only with God are closely interconnected".[13]

We cannot collapse the inbuilt connection between personal and communal prayer. The most remotely contemplative mystic, when praying, is not radically alone, separated from the rest of the Body of Christ. We are united in Christ as his Body. Hence the praying of one member of the body is not disconnected from the rest, but is part of the prayer of the whole body.

In our age where individualistic thinking predominates it is hard for us to think communally. In the present culture people imagine they invent themselves, or re-invent themselves, as they will. By "my" aspirations and "my" decisions I will shape my life, regardless of tradition or communal considerations. In the moral sphere this has led to what Pope Benedict called the "dictatorship of relativism". In a similar way, we are inclined to think of our spiritual life as an individual, personal hot-line to God which has no connection to anyone else.

We need to remember that prayer is a response to God who has first come to us. The way he has come to us, and continues to come to us, must shape our response to him. With immense love and mercy his saving action through history has always been by covenanting himself to a people, not to solitary individuals. In the new covenant by forming us as his people, purchased by the precious blood of Jesus, made one in the Holy Spirit, he has bestowed the wonderful gift of belonging to one another.

When we were baptised, we were not only brought into personal union with Christ, but also into the Body of Christ. In Paul's theology of baptism our union in the Body has primacy. When we are baptised, we are grafted onto the Body of Christ; only in union within the Body do we have life: "Now you together are Christ's body; but each of you is a different part of it" (1Cor 12:27). The "our" of the Lord's prayer expresses this.

We do not go to God alone. We are joined with all our brothers and sisters, sharing in their sorrows and joys, their hopes and dreams. This is why the Our Father is the Church's prayer. Consequently, it is at the centre of all ecumenical prayer, since through the Holy Spirit it unites us in one communion of love with the Father, who has revealed his heart to us through Jesus, his Son. Paul says it so well, "There is one Body, one Spirit, just as you were all called into one and the same hope when you were called. There is one Lord, one faith one baptism, and one God who is Father of all, over all, through all and within all" (Eph 4:4-6). No one individual, and no group, no matter how blessed, has exclusive access to the Father.

Interestingly, in the early Church, during the time when adult candidates were being initiated into the faith community, they were taught the Our Father and its meaning. But they were not able to pray it with the community until after they had been baptised and confirmed at the Easter Vigil. Then during the celebration of Eucharist they would have the privilege of joining in the *Our* Father. Having the Spirit of adoption through baptism they now had the privilege of praying this sacred prayer with the whole body. Something of this concept has been restored today in the Rite of Christian Initiation of Adults. The candidates who have been welcomed through the rite of election at the beginning of Lent will before Easter be presented liturgically with the Our Father. This declares that their baptism will make them sons and daughters empowering them to call God *Abba*.

The "our" of the Lord's prayer, like the "us" of the last four petitions, goes even further. It enables us to utter a cry to the Father in union with the whole of humanity, whether they are Christian or not! We voice the cry hidden in the heart of those who do not yet know the living God. As the Catechism instructs us, the Our Father "excludes no one. If we are to say it truthfully, our divisions and oppositions have to be overcome".[14] This is a radically inclusive prayer. God's graciousness is not confined to members of the Church. We ask for God's kingdom to come to all, for his will to be done throughout the world, that bread will be available for all, that forgiveness would bring reconciliation, and we would all be delivered from evil. Jesus tells us we will only be "sons and daughters of your Father in heaven" when we love our enemies and pray for those who persecute us (Mt 5:45). Nothing could be more inclusive than that. So when we say "our" we recognize that he is Father of all humankind, even if people do not know him; the Father "causes his sun to rise on bad persons as well as good, and his rain to fall on the honest and dishonest alike" (Mt 5:45).

Who art in Heaven

These words are not meant to distance us from God, relegating him to a foreign dimension. Heaven is not an expression of space or place, but of a state of being. It is the ultimate end of our earthly pilgrimage, and the ultimate experience of God, Father, Son and Holy Spirit forever. To the extent that we experience God's grace now we are already in touch with heaven. In every Eucharistic celebration heaven touches earth and in our worship we are drawn into the heavenly liturgy. Earlier we dwelt upon Teresa of Avila's insight that the indwelling presence of God within us is already a taste of heaven. We already possess an anticipation of the fullness yet to come for which the heart yearns. Elizabeth of the Trinity expresses it beautifully:

> It seems to me that I have found my Heaven on earth, because my Heaven is God, and God is in my soul. The day I understood that, everything became clear to me.[15]

The contemplative tradition makes us aware that heaven is already present within us. Jesus himself told us "when you pray go to your private room and, when you have shut your door, pray to your Father who is in the secret place, and your Father who sees all that is done in secret will reward you" (Mt 6:6). Regardless of whether Jesus was originally referring to an actual room in a house, the spiritual tradition has consistently interpreted this as an invitation into the inner cell of the heart to encounter the living God. The Father is not waiting for us in some realm beyond our human experience. Because of the incarnation, through the saving work of Jesus, and the indwelling of the Spirit, in so far as we take the inner contemplative journey we experience heaven now.

Nevertheless, praying to our Father "in heaven" also acknowledges his utter transcendence, his otherness, his majesty. While he is not "elsewhere" he transcends everything that we could imagine holiness would look like. All the concepts and images we may blithely use limp badly before the reality of the living God. The prophet Isaiah's vision in the Temple of the angels singing "Holy, holy, holy" reduced him to cry out "I am a man of unclean lips" (Is 6:5). He knew he was unworthy of such a theophany, deeply aware of his utter nothingness, sinfulness and weakness, and needing purification. Encountering the living God is like this. The language of intimacy with the Father, which shows us so much about what God is like, still leaves us with infinitely more we do *not* know and cannot understand. As Paul says:

> O the depth of the riches and wisdom and knowledge of God! How unsearchable are his judgements and how inscrutable his ways! For who has known the mind of the Lord? Or who has been his counsellor?" (Rom 11:33-34)

This infinite mystery of God's transcendence need not disconcert us. Nor should it dissuade us from opening our hearts to his personal love for us. He has proven his love by Christ dying for us while we were still sinners (Rom 5:8). After such a gift we can be passionate in our response to this love. When we pray "our Father who art in heaven" we are boldly claiming what Jesus has won for us. Out of love for us the Father has "raised us up and seated us with him in the heavenly places in Christ Jesus" (Eph 2:6). Because we were raised with Christ through baptism we must "seek the things that are above, where Christ is seated at the right hand of God". We are to break with inordinate attachments to the things of this world and set our hearts on higher things. Our life now is "hidden with Christ in God" (Col 3:

1-4). Paul is not speaking spatially here as if heavenly existence is on some distant planet. Rather it is a new way of being in which we are caught up in the life of God, not governed by our unruly passions or the allurement of sin.

Finally, addressing the Father "who art in heaven" reminds us of the end of our earthly pilgrimage. In this earthly state we long for our heavenly homeland. We live in a condition now of "already" having tasted something of heaven, but "not yet" having been brought to completion. Our taste of heaven now is nothing compared to what is to come. Paul likens our bodily existence to a tent. He says "in this tent we groan, longing to be clothed with our heavenly dwelling" (2Cor 5:2). The whole of creation, he says, is "groaning in travail", longing for its completion. And we too "groan inwardly while we wait for the redemption of our bodies" (Rom 8:22-23). The author of Hebrews, reflecting on the journey of Abraham and many of the people of old who lived by faith, deduces they were ultimately but pilgrims in this world, not finding here their lasting dwelling place. They were "longing for a better homeland, their heavenly homeland" (Heb 11:15-16). That is our journey also, yearning for the fullness of God yet to come, putting our trust not in the things of this world but in God who is our ultimate end.

HALLOWED BE THY NAME

This first petition, literally speaking, is asking that God's name be held holy. This can at first seem strange, since surely God is holiness itself, and only he can make his name holy. But what is meant here is not that God may be made holy by our efforts at prayer, but that his name may be "hallowed" *in us* and *by us*. The first way this happens in us is through praising God at all times. In praying "hallowed be thy name" we are actually joining the angels in Isaiah's vision, crying "Holy, Holy, Holy is the Lord, God most high!" (Is 6:3). We have already noted how Teresa of Avila highlighted this meaning. It is also the primary way I personally experience this petition. We are full of awe and wonder at the magnificence of God. The petition becomes praise. Secondly, God's name will be held holy to the extent that *we* become holy. We give glory to God through our holiness of life. So we pray for the grace for all men and women to become truly holy, and hence give glory to God. This second meaning is probably the main way the spiritual tradition has interpreted the petition[16]. But it is simply an extension of the previous meaning, since a life of holiness is a prolonged act of praising God's glory. We ask daily to be sanctified, made holy, transformed into the likeness of Jesus as sons and daughters of God. God's name will be glorified to the extent that we take the journey of genuine discipleship. We cannot take one step forward in holiness without the grace of God, so we beg him that through our transformation he will be truly glorified. The third meaning is that God's name be held holy through the way we reverence his name in speech and writing, never using his name lightly or disparagingly. As the second commandment requires, we pray that his name is always held in high esteem and never used in a blasphemous manner.

God Has Given His Name

Before looking further at these three meanings, we need firstly to explore more what is meant by "the name of God". We are familiar with Moses in the desert encountering the living God's presence manifest in a burning bush, which was not consumed. Moses was looking after his sheep and he saw this phenomenon of a thornbush alight with a fire that was not destroying it. He was drawn by curiosity to have a closer look. Then to his great surprise he heard a voice calling him from the middle of the bush. "Moses! Moses! Come no nearer. Take off your shoes. For the place you are standing is holy ground. I am the God of your fathers, the God of Abraham, the God of Isaac, and the God of Jacob" (Ex 3:6). The Lord tells Moses he has heard the cry of the people of Israel who are in bondage in Egypt. He says to Moses, "Go, I send you to Pharaoh to bring the sons of Israel, my people, out of Egypt". Moses is perplexed and reluctant to go back to the Israelites and limply declare, "the God of your fathers has sent me to you". He asks God to reveal his name.

We must remember that Moses lived in a world of many gods. If the God of his fathers was to give his name to Moses so readily, it would put him on par with all these other gods. But the God of his fathers is the one true God, the God of gods, the Lord of lords. So God's answer to Moses is both a refusal and a solemn promise. He simply says YHWH – "I am who I am". His existence is not qualified. It is the expression of ultimate transcendence over any other claims to be god. The Israelites would not utter this name because to do so would bring the one true God into some sort of competition with other gods. They did not want the name of God to be degraded vis a vis the pagan deities.

Yet the fact that God gave a name at all to Moses means that already God is offering access to him. A name "creates the possibility of address or invocation. It establishes relationship".[17] By giving Moses his name, even though mysterious and unutterable, he was opening up a new level of relationship with his people. The one who is above all gods, YHWH, is the one who will be with his people in history, as he had already been with Abraham, Isaac, and Joseph. "This is my name forever, by this name I shall be invoked for all generations to come" (Ex 3:15). At this decisive moment God gives us his name which then comes to completion in Jesus. At the Last Supper Jesus prays to the Father, "I have made your name known to those who you gave me from the world" (Jn 17:6). The new access and intimacy which Jesus gives to us by disclosing the name of the Father makes God even more vulnerable to us. He has, as it were, put himself into our hands.

Praise the Name of the Lord

I have said my preferred way to interpret this petition is to understand it as an act of praise. The gift of praise and adoration springs from within the heart of the Church. The Holy Spirit stirs us to exalt God from the depth of our being. As we worship him we offer ourselves as a "living sacrifice of praise to God" (Rom 12:1). In our assemblies we "sing psalms and hymns and inspired songs to God" (Col 3:16), and then at all times we "go on singing and chanting to the Lord in our hearts" (Eph 5:19). The more the Spirit moves us to worship we experience in a new way the "Holy, Holy, Holy" sung by the angels in Isaiah's vision and included in the Eucharistic liturgy. How can we not praise God for his holiness! To pray "Hallowed be thy name!" is a word of praise, not only petition!

St Augustine starts his Confessions by both praising God and calling upon him. He is not sure which movement goes first; and seems to conclude that they are simply different movements of the one symphony of prayer. Even though human beings are broken and sinful, which provokes a cry for help, they also desire to praise the living God. Addressing God, Augustine exclaims:

> You prompt us to take delight in praising you, because you made us for yourself, and our hearts are restless until they rest in you. Grant me, Lord, to know and understand whether I should first call upon you, or praise you, and to know you before I call on you....[18]

In seeking the Lord we are also praising him. Both go together. As Augustine concludes, "And they shall praise the Lord who seek him, for if they seek him they find him, and finding him they shall praise him".[19]

When we are caught up in praise of God, we join the heavenly host around the throne of God, singing "Holy, Holy, Holy is the Lord, the Almighty, he was, he is and he is to come" (Rev 4:8). In Eucharist, as we worship at the time of the Sanctus, we join in this heavenly liturgy. Together at the table of the Lord we extol his name as holy. And again, when God's people gather to worship spontaneously outside of liturgy, we can't help but be full of awe and wonder at his holiness. We are lifted in worship, and break forth in wordless sounds extolling God for the wonder of his holiness. We "hallow" the name of God. Holy is his name forever and ever! Our praises are not adding to his holiness, but arise out of being overwhelmed by his splendour which we can only grasp in a partial and passing way. But even a glimpse of his glory is enough to lift us beyond ourselves and our paltry existence into a new space of worship, yielding ourselves to the living God who is shrouded in mystery but pouring his love into our hearts.

We are designed to praise God. That is what we will be doing forever in heaven. Petition and praise arise in the heart together. In our weakness and brokenness we know that we are totally reliant on God's mercy, which is the highest quality of his heart. Knowing our petition for holiness is being answered as sheer gift from on high, we cannot but lose ourselves in worship of his majesty. And as we exalt him for his holiness, caught up in the majesty and splendour of our saving God, we cannot but desire deeper union with him. Consequently we must plead for deeper intimacy with him personally, and for his kingdom and his righteousness to come to the earth.

Worship of the Living God

Holy is his name! Not only the name of the Father, but also of the Son. What a beautiful name we have in Jesus! His is the name by which we have been saved from our sins, delivered from the evil one, and set free to live a new life in God. The Lamb that was slain has victory gained. "Victory to God, who sits on the throne, and to the Lamb!" (Rev 7:10) "The Lamb that was sacrificed is worthy to be given power, riches, wisdom, strength, honour, glory and blessing" (Rev 5:12). The whole of creation joins in a wonderful symphony of praise crying, "To the One who is sitting on the throne and to the Lamb, be all praise, honour, glory and power, for ever and ever" (Rev 5:13-14).

The image in Revelations of twenty four elders around the throne of God is riveting. They are all seated on thrones surrounding the mighty throne of God. Each is wearing a golden crown on their heads.

There are flashes of lightning and peals of thunder emanating from the throne of God. Every time the whole host of heaven give thanks to the One sitting on the throne, the elders prostrate themselves before him and worship him. They throw down their crowns in front of the throne, saying, "You are our Lord and our God, you are worthy of glory, honour and power, because you made all the universe and it was only by your will that everything was made and exists" (Rev 4:11).

What a wonderful scene! Notice that they "throw down their crowns". Before the living God there is no other fitting response than to throw down your crown in worship. In creating us, God "crowned" us with glory and honour (Ps 8:6), and we look forward to the "crown of righteousness" prepared for those who run the race to the finish (2 Tim 4:8). During our earthly pilgrimage maybe we have been "crowned" with godly holiness. No matter what the nature of our crown, before the throne of God we readily throw it down before him. Fascinated with his beauty, awe-struck by his Majesty, enraptured in his love, we prostrate ourselves: "Who shall not fear and glorify your name, O Lord? For you alone are holy" (Rev 15:4).

The Our Father, then, is not only a cry for help from our loving God, but is also heartfelt worship of him for his goodness and kindness towards us. We are the people who praise God in all circumstances, especially in times of adversity. Like Paul and Silas in a Philippian gaol, after having been severely lashed, now bound hand and foot, under heavy guard; they did not succumb to despair, but to the contrary turned their hearts to the Lord, most high: "Late that night Paul and Silas were praying and singing God's praises, while the other prisoners listened" (Acts 16:25). Suddenly there was an earthquake. The prison doors flew open, and the chains fell from the prisoners!

When we get our focus off ourselves and our troubles, and when we turn to the Lord and exalt his holy name, we find new liberation;

hope rises in the heart. Holy is your name, Lord God Almighty! Our future is in the hands of the living God who is totally trustworthy. With all the heavenly beings in Revelations we join in the praise which "day and night they never stop singing":

> Holy, Holy, Holy
>
> is the Lord God, the Almighty;
>
> He was, he is and he is to come. (Rev 4:8)

Becoming Holy

Praising God at all times means a commitment to glorify God's name by living righteous lives in imitation of Jesus. This is the second meaning of the petition. Jesus prays to the Father "keep those you have given me true to your name" (Jn 17:12). Jesus is beseeching the Father that we would remain true to him, and be faithful in our journey of discipleship no matter what pressures we experience from the world. We will be totally committed to seeking holiness and persevere in the hard work of personal transformation.

His name is blasphemed when we live in opposition to his ways.[20] We are asking for his holiness to grow in us, and also in others who do not yet know him. We want his name to be blessed throughout the earth by everyone without exception. This has been God's purpose from the beginning. Paul tells us God the Father "chose us in Christ before the foundation of the world to be holy and blameless before him in love", and we were destined from the beginning to be adopted as children of God, "to the praise of his glorious grace that he freely bestowed on us in the Beloved" (Eph 1:4-5).

Quoting from Leviticus, Peter reminds us that the Lord says, "Be holy, for I am holy" (1 Pet1:15; cf. Lev 20:7). This does not mean necessarily becoming a monk or a professional religious. It simply means being formed into the likeness of Jesus who is the Holy One of God. Consequently, the word "holy" carries the meaning of being "set apart", i.e. separated from the worldly influences that distract us from being captivated by the kingdom of God; breaking from the power of the flesh with its self-centred demands; repenting of all sinful patterns and claiming the victory of Jesus; and warding off the temptations of the evil one. Only God is holy. To the extent that we allow him to dwell within us and bring change, we become holy. He wants to recreate us so that we shine with the radiance of his light in the world today. We are a "chosen race, a royal priesthood, a consecrated nation, a people set apart to sing the praises of God" (1 Pet 2:9).

How much have we allowed ourselves to be captured by the Lord's love so that we are authentically becoming like Jesus? Only he can make us holy. By cooperating with the sanctifying work of his Spirit within us we can change. The Lord is a jealous lover. He wants us for himself and will not rest until we truly belong to him. By acknowledging him as Lord of our lives and allowing him to claim us for himself we surrender to the purifying work of his Spirit and gradually we find that the fruits of the Spirit will become evident in our lives. It's not enough to have the language of Christianity, and engage in religious practices. We need to submit to a continually deeper conversion of heart which will increase in us fruits of the Spirit: love, joy, peace, patience kindness and self-control (Gal 5:22).

Giving Glory to God

God's purpose in creating us out of love was that we would give glory and honour to him by our lives. In Genesis we are told God created human beings in his own image and likeness, and "with glory and honour he crowned them" (Ps 8:5). But humankind fell in Adam. Consequently all humanity "fell short of the glory of God" (Rom 3:23). We became dysfunctional as human beings. Our natural powers of intellect, will, memory and imagination were wounded and impaired by original sin. We were no longer able to act in a God-like manner. No matter how much we tried by our own efforts it was not possible to be restored.

God's plan of salvation was to restore us to be able to give glory to him again. God is about a work of "image-restoration" so we could again reflect his glory as a "new creation" in Christ. We are being restored to our original dignity and beauty through the work of the Holy Spirit. This happens through the redeeming power of Jesus Christ who having died on the Cross for our sins and now risen, pours out his Holy Spirit upon us. The Holy Spirit is the holiness of God. His indwelling presence brings transformation making us holy. But we must cooperate with this sanctifying work of the Spirit. By saying "yes" again and again to our baptism, the Holy Spirit applies to us the redeeming power of the death and resurrection of Jesus, changing us into his likeness. By the Spirit we are being changed into the image of Christ "from one degree of glory to another" (2 Cor 3:18). Paul encourages the Colossians by reminding them, "You have stripped off your old self with its practices and have clothed yourselves with the new self, which is being renewed in knowledge according to the image of its Creator" (Col 3:10). The recreating work of the Spirit makes us once again reflect the glory of God as a new creation.

Reverence for the Name

The third meaning of this petition is a commitment not to misuse the name of God in our speech. It reminds us of the second commandment, "You shall not speak the name of the Lord your God in vain". The name of God is so regularly misused in our present culture, not only by words of blasphemy but through words of disbelief which are an affront to the truth, goodness and mercy of God. In our prayer we are asking for the grace of conversion for all non-believers, and especially those who revile God's name and speak of him with contempt. But we are also asking for the courage to uphold his name in times of confrontation and persecution. And beyond our own efforts we are calling upon the Father Almighty to act in whatever way is necessary to defend and protect his name from being besmeared by so many.

We pray that we ourselves will not be guilty of dishonouring his name, or taking advantage of the way he has chosen to be so vulnerable with us. Positively it is a commitment on our part, if we are to pray this petition honestly, that we would never sully the name of God, and we would grow in deep reverence for God's holy name. To pray this petition authentically we need to be growing in reverence before the living God, worshipping in the liturgy with genuine filial fear of God, engaging in the sacred mysteries with awe and wonder, grateful that the almighty God would deign to communicate with us in such a vulnerable way. This comes to a particular poignancy with the Eucharist. Just like Moses trembling before the burning bush, we too must as it were, take off our shoes in reverence before Jesus in the Blessed Sacrament and never become off-handed, over-familiar or indifferent before this sacred mystery.

Reverence for the Eucharistic Presence

Unfortunately, all too often Catholics today can show a lackadaisical attitude towards the real presence of Jesus in the Eucharist. Born out of ignorance, people can show little reverence and fail to appreciate the awesome gift of the body, blood, soul and divinity of the Risen Christ present under the appearance of bread. Bishop Fulton Sheen, the famous American television evangelist has given a compelling witness of reverence for Jesus in the Eucharist.[21] He had a life-time dedication to a holy hour before the Blessed Sacrament each day, and held to it faithfully. Towards the end of his life he was asked who inspired him to undertake such a commitment. He responded that it was not a pope, a cardinal, another bishop, or even a priest or a nun, but rather an eleven year old Chinese girl.

When the communists took over a particular town in China, they imprisoned a priest in his own presbytery near the church. Locked in his own house, the priest was horrified when from his window he saw the communists enter the church. They went into the sanctuary, broke open the tabernacle and threw the ciborium to the floor scattering the consecrated hosts. The priest knew how many hosts were in the tabernacle – exactly 39.

When the communists left they didn't see a small girl who had been praying in the back of the church. That night the girl returned, avoiding the guard and going into the church. She fell to her knees for a "holy hour" before the Blessed Sacrament which was still strewn all over the floor. After her "holy hour" she bent over and with her tongue received one of the hosts. At that time lay people could not touch the host with their hands, so she consumed Jesus in the only way possible to her.

Each night the girl would return, watched silently by the priest from his window. She would make her "holy hour" and then consume another of the desecrated hosts. On the thirty-ninth night she slipped past the guard as usual and went through her ritual. But after consuming the last host, as she was leaving, she stumbled and woke up the guard. The priest watched helplessly as the guard chased her and, having caught her, bludgeoned her to death with the butt of his rifle. A martyr's death of a girl whose name will never be known, but a witness to the holy name of Jesus, which inspired Bishop Sheen to make a "holy hour" before the Blessed Sacrament for the rest of his life.

The Only Name by which we can be Saved

"Hallowed be thy name" on Jesus' lips was originally referring to the Father. But in a derivative way it refers also to reverence for the name of Jesus, the incarnate Son, and also for the name of the Holy Spirit. When entering a church we dip our hand in holy water and bless ourselves. A reminder of our baptism in the name of the Father, the Son and Holy Spirit (Mt 28). To "hallow" the name of God is to hold all three names of the persons of the Trinity to be holy. When we reverence the name of Jesus we give glory to the Father also. When we reverence the Holy Spirit we give glory to Jesus.

In Jesus, the name of the Holy God is given to us in the flesh. The name, *Jesus*, reveals the name of God, the *"one who saves"*. The name of God is revealed by who Jesus is, the word he proclaims and what he does. The name of Jesus, the incarnate Son of God, carries with it all the authority and power of the living God. To invoke the name of Jesus is to call upon his presence and power right here and now. When the apostles returned from their first missionary journey, they excitedly reported to Jesus, "Lord, even the devils submit to us when we use your name" (Lk 10: 17). This was only a foretaste of what they were to experience after the name of the Father had been glorified through Jesus' death and resurrection (Jn 18:28). After Pentecost, by the working of the Spirit, the apostles preached in the name of

Jesus, cast out demons in his name, healed the sick in his name, and performed all sorts of signs and wonders in his name. To invoke the name of Jesus meant to be assured of the powerful presence of the Risen Lord, continuing his ministry which began in Galilee and had now become universal in scope and impact.

The Name above all Names

The religious authorities quickly realized they had to stop the name of Jesus being invoked. The power in the name was only too blatantly evident. Peter and John going up to the Temple had met a man crippled from birth being carried towards his regular begging spot before the Beautiful Gate. With the man begging from them, Peter and John told him "Look at us". The man turned towards them and Peter said, "I have neither silver nor gold, but I will give you what I have. In the name of Jesus Christ the Nazarene, walk". The man got up and began walking, jumping and praising God. A crowd quickly gathered and Peter began to preach.

Word of the healing travelled like wild fire, and many people were being converted. The religious authorities panicked, quickly reining in Peter and John, and demanding, "By what power, and by whose name have you done this?" Peter gladly answered, "It was by the name of Jesus Christ the Nazarene, the one you crucified, whom God raised from the dead, by this name and no other that this man is able to stand up perfectly healthy, here in your presence today…for of all the names in the world, this is the only one by which we can be saved" (Acts 4:7-10).

The hymn in Philippians expresses this beautifully:
> God raised him from the dead and gave him the name which
> is above every other name. Now at the name of Jesus every

knee shall bow in heaven and on earth and in the underworld, and every tongue confess that Jesus Christ is Lord to the glory of God the Father. (Phil 2: 9-11)

The name of Jesus is to be held precious within our hearts and never used loosely, but always with respect and reverence. His name is powerful, to be honoured, and to be used with faith. I always shrink when I hear the name of Jesus used unthinkingly in banter or jokes, but more so when it is used blasphemously. Many have died for their faith with that name on their lips. How could we trivialise it?

Witness of Martyrs

I was touched by the video of the Coptic martyrs who were beheaded at the merciless hand of ISIS on a beach along the southern Mediterranean coast in February 2016. They were mainly young Christian men, and many could be heard in their last moments calling on the name of Jesus. The Bishop of Giza, Antonios Aziz Mina, commented poignantly, "The name of Jesus was the last word on their lips. And like the early Church martyrs they entrusted themselves to the one who would receive them soon after. That name, whispered in the last moments, was like the seal of martyrdom".[22]

This reminded me of the early Jesuit martyrs in North America in the eighteenth century.[23] Isaac Jogues and lay brother, Rene Goupil, had been captured by the fearsome Mohawk Indians and enslaved within a large village named Ossernon. They had made a pact with one another that whenever they would be put to death, which could happen at any time, they would die with the name of Jesus on their lips. The fateful moment came for Rene, a lay brother, when a young Indian brave for no reason hacked his head open with a tomahawk. Isaac recorded the death in his diary with great joy, since Rene had been true to his promise and uttered the name of Jesus with his last breath. Isaac's time was to come much later, but he too was faithful to the pact.

When instructing his apostles before ascending to the Father, Jesus opened their minds to understand that the purpose of God, shown through the law and prophets, was that the Christ would suffer and rise from the dead, "and *in his name* repentance for the forgiveness of sins would be preached to all the nations" (Lk 24:47). We cannot underestimate the power and authority invested in us in pronouncing the name of Jesus.

Power in the Name

Joseph Chee from Kota Kinabalu in Malaysia some years ago shared a story from their missionary outreach. They were moving through the jungle from one village to another in single file. Suddenly the man in the lead halted, frozen, unable to move. A large cobra had risen up in front of him. He knew that any movement of his would not be quick enough to elude the snake's attack. Trembling and breathless he managed to utter the name of Jesus. With that the cobra folded and slid away into the jungle. When in danger we find protection by invoking the name of Jesus. We know from experience that using his name with faith we can cast out demons and break the power of Satan in people's lives. Jesus promised, "in my name they will cast out devils... they will lay their hands on the sick who will recover" (Mk 16: 17-18).

At the Last Supper Jesus promised his followers, "the Father will give you anything you ask him in my name" (Jn 15:16). When we pray the Our Father we are doing just that, asking him in the name of Jesus, to bring his Kingdom, by empowering us to do his will, to provide our daily bread, to forgive our sins, to protect us from temptation and deliver us from evil. It is a prayer guaranteed to be effective. When we utter this prayer in the name of Jesus we are joined with the heart of Jesus himself, who is forever interceding before us at the throne of the Father in heaven (Heb 8:25). No prayer is more powerful than that.

THY KINGDOM COME

What is God Doing?

A provocative preacher once asked his congregation, "What on earth is God doing for heaven's sake?" After a pregnant pause he delivered the answer, "He is bringing about his kingdom!" This proclamation is at the heart of Jesus' preaching and all his healings, miracles and exorcisms. At the beginning of Mark's gospel we read, "Now after John was arrested, Jesus came into Galilee, preaching the good news of God, 'The time has come' he said, 'and the kingdom of God is at hand; repent and believe the good news!'" (Mk 1:14-15). This is a succinct summary of the whole message of Jesus. The loving reign of God was decisively breaking into history in his person and his actions; the saving presence of God was at hand. This good news is so compelling the only adequate response is to repent and believe.

When we pray "thy kingdom come" we are not asking God to get something started. The kingdom of God is already at hand. We are asking that hearts will open to God's saving love in Jesus, and that we may be instruments for the joyful news of his kingdom to be discovered and embraced by others. "Thy kingdom come!" is not a plaintive call to the Lord for action, as if everything depended on our plea. The decisive action has already happened through Jesus' birth, ministry, death and resurrection. It is more like a "war cry", knowing we are on the winning side.

In my final year in an all boys' high school I was the leader of the "war cry" when the first XV Rugby team were battling against formidable opponents. As our team came onto the field we would let out an almighty shout with great confidence in victory, believing in the "spirit" of the College to give the break-throughs we needed. The analogy may limp a little; but it expresses something of our attitude toward the coming of the kingdom. It is a shout of welcome for the victor King, as we throw our whole being and all our energy behind the saving work of God for the world. It could even be likened to a battle cry of an army before engaging the enemy. Think of the famous call to battle depicted in the film *Braveheart*, when 13th century Scottish warrior, William Wallace, stirred his men to a roar of victory as they engaged the forces assembled against them. We have utter confidence that victory is ours! Not because of us, but because of what Jesus has already done. The battle may still be raging, but we know we already have the victory.

Victory in Christ

Of course, the kingdom of God does not admit of violence, nor is the enemy flesh and blood. Rather we battle against "the spiritual army of evil in the heavens" (Eph 6: 10-13). But, most importantly, Jesus has already had the victory. During his preaching and ministry Jesus engaged in battle with Satan and all the powers of evil. Through his many exorcisms the kingdom of light was decisively overcoming the kingdom of darkness. This victory was definitively won through Jesus' death and resurrection. Just before his passion he proclaimed, "Now sentence has been passed on this world, now the prince of this world is to be overthrown. And when I am lifted up from the earth I will draw all to myself" (Jn 12: 31-32). This prophecy was fulfilled when he was "lifted up" on the Cross on Calvary, and then by the Father in resurrection. He won for us the total victory over hatred by his sacrifice of love. Evil was overcome by goodness and vengeance was met with forgiveness. This is the victory into which we are baptised.

This drama of salvation becomes effective for us when we accept what Christ has done for us. In prayer meetings in Papua New Guinea the locals enthusiastically belt out a victory song celebrating "Jesus, the Winner-Man". This is what we are doing when we cry "thy kingdom come"! We are expressing our faith that Jesus has won the victory; "the gates of hell" will not prevail against the Church as long as we are faithful to preaching the kingdom of God and live accordingly.

The Hebrew word for kingdom, *malkut*, and its Greek translation, *basileia*, refer to the active rule of a king amongst his people. It is not referring to a geographical "kingdom" that could be located on a map, like earthly rulers possess. Nor does it refer to a cause or an ideology. It is about God's saving work in the world today; the reign of God's love taking hold in the hearts of men and women, creating a new way of being together for the sake of further proclaiming this good news. The kingdom of God was prepared for in the Old Testament, inaugurated in the ministry of Jesus, accomplished through his death and resurrection, actualised in this time of the Church's preaching, and will be consummated when the Lord comes again in glory. We live now through the power of the Spirit in the time of the Church. The kingdom is *already* upon us but *not yet* fully realized.

Jesus and the Kingdom

The kingdom was revealed in the person of Jesus, through his words and actions. Jesus lived to inaugurate the kingdom and died for the kingdom to be accomplished. When he opened the eyes of the blind, made the deaf hear and the dumb speak, freed the lame to walk and raised the dead, he was giving clear signs of his messianic presence ushering in the kingdom of God. These were signs of the new rule of God's liberating love taking hold in history.

Pope John Paul II stressed how the kingdom is totally centred in Jesus and cannot be seen apart from him:

> The Kingdom of God is not a concept, a doctrine, or a program subject to free interpretation, but is before all else a person with the face and name of Jesus of Nazareth, the image of the invisible God. If the kingdom is separated from Jesus, it is no longer the kingdom of God which he revealed.[24]

This is an important corrective to some contemporary uses of the "kingdom of God" as if it had nothing to do with Jesus. In secularised thinking the "kingdom" becomes a symbol for harnessing all the energies of humankind toward a future world governed by peace, justice and conservation of creation. All religions will work together to bring about this better world. This is a noble aspiration but how can it be attained without Christ? When we pray "thy Kingdom come" we are not just praying for a better world through human wisdom and collective cooperation. Certainly we want more common work for the good of humanity. But it would be a mistake to take Christ out of the picture. It is not enough to live by a secularist interpretation of the kingdom. Good works alone do not bring salvation. We must surrender to the primacy of the Spirit of God and move as he leads us.

When the early Christians began to preach under the power of the Spirit given at Pentecost they simply proclaimed, "Christ is Risen!" and "Jesus is Lord!" The kingdom of God preached by Jesus had been accomplished in his death and resurrection. Now in post-resurrection preaching the Scriptural language changes. His followers under the anointing of the Spirit proclaim in the name of Jesus that he is alive!

He is the Lord of all! Salvation is for those who will accept him as their Lord. Christians proclaimed unashamedly that the Risen Christ was acting now and showing himself in history in and through the actions of his disciples. Through the proclamation of the kerygma by the apostles the kingdom of God preached by Jesus of Nazareth was now taking place.

Their message was simple. Jesus who was put to death for our sins was raised by the Father, and this Jesus is Lord of all. He acts through the community of his disciples especially when they invoke his name bringing signs and wonders and convincing unbelievers to repent and put their faith in God. When we pray "thy kingdom come" we are asking for the prayer of Paul to be fulfilled: that "every knee shall bow and every tongue confess that Jesus Christ is Lord to the glory of God the Father" (Phil 2:10-11).

The Time has Come

To announce the good news of the kingdom of God is to proclaim salvation has come to the world in Jesus Christ. Now is the *kairos* moment; the anointed and appointed time of God's in-breaking redeeming action in and for the world. Liberation from the power of sin and from bondage to the evil one has come. Eternal life is available for all who believe in Jesus as the Son of God. In the incarnate Word, God has drawn near to us. That is why it is the "fullness of time"; why this is the unique moment like none other, a time for repentance and genuine conversion, a time of joy because God's rule has come. God is acting in a decisive way, breaking into history, changing hearts, not using worldly power but capturing hearts by his love and winning them to himself.

When Jesus tells the crowds the kingdom of God does not admit of observation, he says it will not be a matter of saying, "here it is" or "there it is". Rather he says, "the kingdom of God is in your midst" (Lk 17:20). Some translations say "the kingdom of God is *within* you". This carries some of the meaning, since it is certainly true that the kingdom comes about through the grace of God winning hearts and our whole hearted response to his invitation of love. However, maybe it is more accurate to stay with the translation "in your midst". Maybe Jesus is simply saying the kingdom is coming about "through me as I stand before you". He identifies himself with the kingdom. This interpretation is similar to the words he says in refuting the Pharisees' contention that he is possessed, "If it is by the finger of God that I cast out devils then the kingdom of God is upon you" (Lk 11:20). Yes, his ministry of deliverance spoke powerfully of the reality that Satan's kingdom was being routed. The kingdom of light was overcoming the darkness. A decisively new authority had come to the earth in the person of Jesus, the incarnate Son of God.

Kingdom and Church

To ask "thy kingdom come" we are praying that the Church would be true to its mission in the world today. The Church is a sign and anticipation of the kingdom of God. To the extent that we are true to our vocation, a culture of the kingdom of God can be found within the community of the disciples, a way of life which is characterised by relationships of acceptance and love, healing and forgiveness, practical love and compassion for the sinner and outcast, a love for the poor, a welcome for the marginalised, and the joyful proclamation of the good news of Jesus to all. This is the primary way the kingdom of God will be advanced in the world.

In praying "thy kingdom come" we are praying for preachers

to proclaim boldly the truth of Jesus' death and resurrection, for teachers to expound the faith with clarity, for pastors to care for their flock with compassion, for evangelists to reach out to the lost and alienated with the merciful heart of Jesus, for the whole community of disciples to be a joyful witness of the new life we have found in Jesus, the Risen Lord. We are praying for a new culture which speaks of the values of the kingdom, a culture of life and love, of mercy and unconditional acceptance in which justice and peace are found.

To pray "thy kingdom come" we are acknowledging the primacy of God in the affairs of this world. Where God is not recognised this is a loss for humanity. If God is absent then nothing good can happen. Jesus told us, "seek first his kingdom and his righteousness, and all these things shall be yours as well" (Mt 6:33). In praying for the kingdom to come we want priorities to be right; that God be honoured and we depend on him for everything. We want God to reign in our own lives and in the lives of others. We want human pride to be broken and arrogance abandoned; that the whole of humanity give Lordship to Jesus Christ to the glory of God the Father.

When the Pharisees tried to trick Jesus by asking "Is it permissible to pay taxes to Caesar or not?", they thought they had him trapped. If he said yes it would seem he favoured the occupying power. If he said no it would put him in danger with the Romans. Instead he asked for a coin, had them identify the image of Caesar on the coin, and replied, "Give back to Caesar what belongs to Caesar, and give to God what belongs to God" (Mt 22:21). Yes, we should pay taxes and recognise legitimate authority, but in reality everything belongs to God. We will only worship the living God, no other authority.

The early Christians in proclaiming Jesus is Lord (*kurios* in Greek), were putting things straight. In the Roman Empire it was customary to say "Caesar is *kurios*" since the Emperor was seen as the ultimate ruler of the world. To the contrary, Christians were proclaiming that in fact Jesus Christ, risen from the dead, and seated at right hand of the Father is truly Lord! They would bow down before no other, even if it meant sacrifice of their lives in martyrdom.

The Joy of the Kingdom

To welcome the kingdom of God is an experience of the love of God capturing our hearts. Opening ourselves to his overwhelming love we find immeasurable joy flooding our being. We are like the man in the parable who found the hidden treasure. It filled him with such joy that he gave up everything so he could possess this prize. Similarly in the parable of the pearl of great price Jesus promises joy beyond telling (Mt 13:44-46). The kingdom of God is a reign of merciful love. We witness the joy of Matthew who Jesus looked upon with such mercy and called him regardless of his shady past (Mt 9:9). We see in the parable of the prodigal son the joy brought by the father's embrace and then later the words of the father to the older son who resented his father's large-heartedness: "we had to celebrate and rejoice, because this brother of yours was dead and has come back to life; he was lost and is found" (Lk 15:32). The kingdom of God surprises us with joy in this life and will do so in its fullness yet to come.

Jesus shows his own joy especially with repentant sinners. He happily eats with sinners and outcasts; his mercy is for them and wants to bring them forgiveness and peace. The Pharisees are scandalised by his actions, but Jesus is undeterred. "There is more joy in heaven over one repentant sinner than over ninety nine who had no need of repentance" (Lk 15:7). A classic story is that of Zacchaeus, a senior tax collector in Jericho. He had become rich by a contract with the Roman occupying power, which allowed him to set his own commission and defraud people in collecting revenue.

Despised by his fellow Jews for collaborating with the Romans, Zacchaeus was secretly drawn out of curiosity to try and catch a glimpse of Jesus from a safe perch in an overhanging sycamore tree. But Jesus stopped, looked up and called him by name, "Zacchaeus hurry and come down, for I must stay at your place tonight". This encounter with mercy, as he looked into the eyes of Jesus, changed Zacchaeus. He was ready to give generously to those he had cheated and was delighted to welcome Jesus. The kingdom was taking hold in his heart. Jesus rejoices, "Today salvation has come to this house...... for the Son of man has come to seek and save the lost" (Lk 19:1-10).

Kingdom Moments

Wherever Jesus is present his kingdom of love and mercy is coming about. When grace breaks into our lives, the goodness of God is experienced, and the new power of the kingdom takes hold.

An elderly, faithful dying woman with her children around her in a hospital ward, receives the last sacraments. Unable to speak, struggling to breathe, wide eyes focussed on the priest, absorbing the spiritual comfort, from nowhere finds the words, "Thank you Jesus".

A young man, full of bitterness towards his father, who had abused his sister and bashed his mother, finds the grace in the midst of a healing session to utter "In your name, Jesus, I forgive him". Tears flow; his whole body relaxing as he yields to the healing love of God.

A young woman who never knew her father and could not express her love for her mother, having fallen into destructive relationships with boys, succumbed to the pressure of having an abortion; shattered, deeply lonely, full of loss and grief, sure that no one could possibly understand. She comes to an evangelising weekend, overcome by the love of those around her, drawn to the sacrament of reconciliation, pours out the pain in her heart, and is filled with the love of God; a hard heart melted under love's persuasive touch.

A young wife feeling ostracized from her demanding, critical husband, attends a healing Mass. She is reduced to tears when a word is given that someone in the congregation feels cut to pieces and without hope. Jesus will heal. Receiving prayer afterwards she forgives her husband and discovers a new love she thought impossible.

A married man who has hidden from his wife his addiction to pornography attends a weekend for men. He breaks open in a sharing group; the first time he could be vulnerable and feel safe. Repentance, tears, companionship, encouragement, and new skills to work on his issue, a fresh experience of the Holy Spirit and confidence for the first time that he can have victory in Christ.

A crippled old man, seated on a box outside his shack in a squatter settlement in Manila's worst slums. He meets the pastoral team with a gleaming smile exposing his cracked and broken teeth. He asks for prayer. This is not the first time; the deepest hunger of the human heart is for the love of God. The team explains how some young men are going to strengthen the walls of his home and provide a galvanised iron roof, and they share with him some rice and meat. The smile widens as he receives the offering, but quickly asks for a spiritual blessing. The food is good to receive, but hope in God is the greater gift.

In an adult male detention centre where the majority of prisoners are indigenous, a young man carries his inner pain with no capacity to share or articulate his deep wounding; jailed for many years, what has he to keep him going? When attending "chapel", listening to the gospel he is struck by a word; it pierces his heart. He seeks out the chaplain. He now senses he has a future full of hope, even though he will be behind bars for years to come. All is not lost; God is with him.

The Signs of the Kingdom

When the kingdom of God is taking hold we can joyfully expect signs. When Jesus was asked by messengers from John the Baptist whether he was the Messiah, he answered by pointing to the signs and wonders, "Go back and tell John what you have seen and heard: the blind see again, the lame walk, lepers are cleansed, and the deaf hear, the dead are raised to life, the good news is proclaimed to the poor" (Lk 7:22). When the kingdom of God is at hand we should expect to see and hear signs of this kind happening. We will be moved by physical, emotional and spiritual healings and deliverance.

The saving power of Jesus is primarily about rescuing us from sin and the power of Satan and giving us new life forever. But Jesus makes this evident through healing our physical ailments, strengthening our weak wills, bringing our emotional life into order, restoring us from early traumas, freeing us from undue anxiety, shame and guilt. The good news is not meant to be simply a doctrine, or a truth to be believed. It is meant to be seen and heard through accompanying signs and wonders, which verify the truth of what is proclaimed. When we pray "thy kingdom come" we are asking for the ministry of Jesus to continue in the Church today.

When the seventy-two returned to Jesus from their first missionary journey they were rejoicing that even the devils submitted to them when they used his name. Jesus rejoiced with them. "I watched Satan fall like lightning from heaven" (Lk 10:1-12). They were sharing in Jesus' power over the forces of evil. God's kingly power was breaking the dominion of Satan. Jesus was obviously delighted in what happened during their mission training. In response, "filled with joy by the Holy Spirit", he prayed, "I bless you Father, Lord of heaven and earth, for hiding these things from the learned and clever and revealing them to mere children" (Lk 10:21). Nothing gives greater joy to Jesus than seeing his followers proclaiming the kingdom, not only in words but also in actions.

Let Jesus be Lord

In asking for the kingdom to come we are asking for Jesus, the Christ, to rule in our hearts. We want him to conquer our wills. Where there is resistance we want him to overcome. We are asking for the grace to let Jesus be Lord. If in our hearts we reject Christ's presence, or allow our passions to rule us, or are allured by the attractions of this world, the kingdom will not take root. On the other hand, if we welcome Christ's presence unreservedly, allow him to rule our passions, and let him capture us by his love, the kingdom will begin to grow. To pray for the kingdom to come is to surrender our hearts to his rule of love, to give all to him, to hold nothing back, to yield to his persuasive power, and to allow him dominion over our lives.

We must let him conquer us with his love. In the Song of Songs there is a text, "My Beloved is mine and I am his… and his banner over me is love" (Song 2:16,4). The nuptial imagery evokes a tender, exclusive love, in which we are ready to joyfully surrender ourselves into the intimacy of his embrace. But the "banner" also suggests a military image. In ancient warfare the conquering king would always have his banner planted on the newly won territory to claim it as his own. The image speaks of allowing the Lord to conquer us, not by force, but by the free gift of his infinite and unconditional love, winning us to himself so we freely yield the territory to him. The heart has changed. It is no longer my autonomous territory governed by my will, but now is ruled by the Lord, who is the joy of my life and all I desire. I gladly allow such a wonderful Saviour to rule my heart and I joyfully yield my will to him.

Encounter with Fire

I have come to realise the truth of Paul's words that "the kingdom of God is not about food and drink, but about righteousness, peace and joy brought by the Holy Spirit" (Rom 14:17). In this text Paul was correcting the Roman Christians for preoccupation with Jewish laws about cleanliness of food. Just like we can get caught up judging one another over minuscule issues in ritual or religious practice. We can forget that "alive or dead we belong to the Lord" (Rom 14:8). All that matters is that we encounter Jesus and are fascinated with him. This only happens through the Holy Spirit. We pray to the Father, "thy kingdom come", yearning for more people to know Jesus, not just as a prophet, or a wise man, or a miracle worker, but as the Divine Saviour, without whom we are all lost.

In the early days of youth ministry I became convinced that only the Holy Spirit can make Jesus real for us. There's a huge difference between telling people about the gospel and declaring the good news in the power of the Spirit. We started our endeavours through well-meaning instruction on who Jesus is. We sought to strip away many of the false notions of Christ that young people had acquired either through popular culture or faulty catechesis. All that was good, but lacking in power. Then as we turned to the Lord and begged for his Spirit things began to happen. The kingdom of God was manifest before our very eyes as young people who previously had been somewhat bored and distracted suddenly became electrified by the revelation that Jesus was real. They were actually meeting the Risen Jesus for the first time, even though many had received years of catechism classes already.

Overwhelmed by the love of God their hearts changed and lives were transformed. We discovered that "the kingdom of God is about righteousness, peace and joy brought by the Holy Spirit"! But in a strange way we found it did actually involve "food and drink". But not as Paul was correcting. The faithful Spirit-filled women who came to cook for our evangelising weekends made sure the young people enjoyed many culinary delights, disposing them towards the spiritual food to come! More importantly these wonderful prayer warriors would spend their time interceding for the participants, pleading for the Holy Spirit to fall when we preached and shared our testimonies. Their prayer and fasting opened heaven's gate again and again; a secret that the Church needs to discover in every age.

A Church in Crisis Prays

The Church today has been humbled through the sexual abuse crisis. We are significantly traumatised by what has happened. At the epicentre of this trauma are the many victim-survivors whose lives have been shattered and their relationship with the Church severely damaged. Many other members of the Church have been left bewildered, disillusioned, and feeling alienated from the institution which has failed them. In this unspeakable tragedy we need to find a hidden grace of restoration. We need to become a listening people, ready to sit with those who are suffering most; ready to minister compassion and healing from the heart of Christ.

We need to humble ourselves and repent of our institutional

arrogance and self-protection; we need to come before the Lord of all mercy and together weep for our sins. As we pray "Thy kingdom come" from our broken hearts, we are begging the Lord to forgive us and to touch into our wounded lives with his healing presence. We need to resist the temptation to stand like the Pharisee at the front of the Temple justifying our actions before God and before others; rather it is a time to be with the tax-collector at the back of the Temple, with eyes cast down, trembling with the realisation of our weakness and failure, our brokenness and sinfulness, crying, "Lord, have mercy on me, a sinner". In this way the kingdom of God's mercy and healing may be present in our midst.

A Humble, Servant Church Prays

When we pray for the kingdom of God to be truly manifest in the world through the life of the Church, we must not be self-referential, focussed only on our own development and internal ecclesial issues. Rather than concern for self-preservation, the Church makes the kingdom present when it is thoroughly missionary, with its focus outward towards the world. We are called to be a community of missionary disciples going forward with joyful proclamation.[25]

Mere administration is not enough; we need to be permanently in a state of mission. Our prayer to the Father is not firstly to meet our own needs, or solve our internecine problems, but to enter into the pain, the suffering and the misery of others. As the document on the Church in the Modern World at Vatican II stated so poignantly:

> The joys and hopes, the grief and anguish of the people of our time, especially of those who are poor or afflicted, are the joys and hopes, the grief and anguish of the followers of Christ as well.[26]

Sometimes we hold back due to fear of rejection, ridicule or irrelevance. But the proclamation of Jesus is always "good news" when it is truly lived before words are spoken. It demonstrates the compassion and mercy of God. As Pope Francis says,

> More than fear of going astray, my hope is that we will be moved by the fear of remaining shut up within structures which give us a false sense of security, within rules which make us harsh judges, within habits which make us feel safe, while at the door people are starving and Jesus does not tire of saying to us: "Give them something to eat".[27]

Pope Francis calls for a Church with open doors, "going out to others in order to reach the fringes of humanity"[28] ; a Church that welcomes all into the merciful embrace of the Father. We are not "to be the kind of Christian who keeps the Lord's wounded at arm's length". We are to "touch the suffering flesh of others", showing the reality of God's tenderness.[29] Under a new missionary impulse we must go to everyone without exception. But to whom shall we go first? Pope Francis instructs us to read the gospels for the answer:

> Not so much our friends and wealthy neighbours, but above all the poor and the sick, those who are usually despised and overlooked, 'those who cannot repay you'.[30]

Blessed are the Poor in Spirit

Jesus makes it clear that entry to the kingdom only comes through true poverty of spirit. The first Beatitude sums up all the rest: "Blessed are the poor in spirit; theirs is the kingdom of heaven" (Mt 5:1). When we realize our utter dependence on God for everything, and accept we are incapable of existence without him, we joyfully place ourselves in his hands. Jesus does not mince words: "Unless you change and become like little children you cannot enter the kingdom of heaven" (Mt 18:3). Children are not self-sufficient, but totally reliant on parents for support and nourishment. This is our true state before God.

Unfortunately, we can spend our lives ignoring this truth, building our lives on sand rather than on rock. To welcome the kingdom of God is to recognise our utter vulnerability and total dependence on God. We become blessed if we accept our state as creatures and don't deny this truth as Adam and Eve did. Without poverty in spirit everything goes wrong. This was the original fault of Adam and Eve. In the garden of Eden, they refused to trust the promise of God, and listened rather to the promise of the Evil One. Now in Jesus we can reverse this path. We can put our trust totally in God for everything.

The only authentic way to walk through these few short years on this earth is to hold onto nothing, so that we can hold onto God and be held by him. This is the attitude of detachment. The poor in spirit know that everything is gift from God. They walk through life with a profound sense of gratitude which is the way to humility. When we are grateful we recognise that God is the source of all the gifts of creation and salvation. On the other hand, when we are ungrateful, we complain about our lot and pine for what others have. We fall into envy of others' gifts and possessions.

The authentic journey through adult life is not towards amassing wealth, power, status and honour. Rather it is a way of self-emptying so we can be filled by God's presence. It's is not a way of accumulating more, but of letting go of the reins of our life in favour of God. It is not a way to worldly greatness, but a way to littleness so we can be fashioned as great in God. It is the way of poverty which leads ultimately to the door of death when we enter with utterly nothing, and are welcomed into fullness of life forever. This leads us finally to reflect on the Kingdom to come.

The Kingdom Yet to Come

So far we have mainly meditated on the actualisation of the kingdom in our own lives now and in the Church in these times. But to pray for the coming of the kingdom is not only to ask God to free us to love and worship him in this present age, but also in the age to come. The kingdom of God is coming about now but is yet to be consummated. To pray with Jesus for the kingdom of God is to yearn for the fullness of salvation yet to come, to yearn for when we will be taken into glory. It is to live with expectant faith longing for the coming of the Lord on the clouds of heaven at the end of time.

We don't long for the consummation of the kingdom as if the work we are called to do now on earth has no relevance; as if we only want to look upwards to the heavenly realm. Just as it is a mistake to interpret the building of the kingdom of God as a purely earthly enterprise, so also is it erroneous to look exclusively for the kingdom of God to come in the future, when we die or when he comes to meet us in the *parousia*. We must take responsibility for shaping the world today according to the values of the kingdom. It is important to maintain the eschatological tension between what is *already* happening by God's transforming grace in the world and what is *yet to come* when he returns in glory.

Having made that qualification, we can assert without hesitation that when we pray "thy kingdom come" we are definitely longing for *what is yet to come*; anticipating the moment of our own personal judgment and also the moment of the Lord's coming again in glory for the universal judgment of all humankind. The Spirit within us makes us eager for this completion. Paul tells us "from the beginning the whole creation is groaning in one great act of giving birth" and because we have received the first fruits of the Spirit we too "groan inwardly as we await our redemption" (Rom 8:22-23). We long for that day when what is now hidden will be made manifest. On that day the one who came as the sacrificial lamb for our sake, and has been rejected by many, will come in power and glory on the clouds of heaven. Unmistakably he will be manifest as king before all; beyond any doubt he will rule the world; but unfortunately for many it may be too late.

We pray that the Spirit of God would touch the hearts of those resistant to the Word of God, and those whose choices are leading them on the spacious road to damnation, before it is too late for them (cf. Mt 7:13-14). We want all men and women to be ready and alert to the coming of the Lord. His kingdom is of grace and peace. Then love and mercy will reign. As we long for his coming we don't wish any destruction upon anyone, but rather earnestly cry out for his mercy. At the time of judgement we need not fear; our greatest assurance is of a merciful judgement for every individual, and the gospels indicate there may be more than a few surprises in regard to who is welcomed into heavenly bliss.

Ultimately the measure of our lives will be how we have loved. When Jesus comes in his glory we trust we will hear the words, "Come, you whom my Father has blessed, take for your heritage the kingdom prepared for you since the foundation of the world". But there is a clear condition put on this by Jesus, which should always be cause for sober reflection: "For I was hungry and you gave me food; I was thirsty and you gave me drink; I was a stranger and you made me welcome; naked and you clothed me, sick and you visited me, in prison and you came to see me" (Mt 25: 31-46). To pray "your kingdom come" would be a discordant note and bordering on hypocrisy if we are not now ministering to the wounded flesh of Christ in the distressing disguise of the poor.

THY WILL BE DONE ON EARTH AS IT IS IN HEAVEN

We pray that the loving plan of God for humanity be fully realized on earth as it already is in heaven. "He has let us know the mystery of his purpose, the hidden plan he so kindly made in Christ from the beginning…that he would bring everything together under Christ, as head, everything in the heavens and everything on earth" (Eph 1:9-10). Our prayer is that his plan for the salvation of all people and the restoration of the world will be realized in our days. It is the Father's will that no one will be lost, but all will attain salvation (Mt 18:14). Out of his infinite love for every person, "he wants everyone to be saved and reach full knowledge of the truth" (1Tim 2:4). We are praying for no less than the conversion of every person to Christ, who is the only way to salvation.

However, in every age there has been opposition to God's plan, a refusal to cooperate with his saving will. Our present modern culture is no exception; resistance to God is rampant. God's loving plan of salvation is met with indifference and arrogant self-sufficiency. The prevailing secularised culture shuts God out of daily life and ignores his presence. So many of our contemporaries prefer to walk in the darkness of unbelief, failing to acknowledge their need for God and refusing to submit their lives to his will.

The Cultural Challenge

In the current post-Christian culture individual freedom is unduly exaggerated. The quest for freedom is not bound to truth. People often have no concept of doing the will of God, nor of living out a vocation given from above. They don't want to be accountable to any religious tradition. They revel in being an autonomous individual who is answerable only to oneself. The tendency is to define myself according to my own chosen values and my own way of seeing the world. This dream of unlimited freedom is not in any way based on objective truth or anything revealed by God. It leads to tribalism where groups gather around certain common values. Yet individuals feel free to move at will from one tribe to the next according to their fancy. In this sort of society people cannot find meaning and purpose. Nor can they find right relationship. They are left without an anchor in life. Everything dysfunctions. Only when we desire God and seek the truth will we be able to have right relationships, meaning in life and true freedom.

Mistakenly people think they can create their own identity, invent themselves, and then if that is not pleasing anymore, they proceed to re-invent themselves. The Christian journey is different. I find who I am in God and discover the truth through the Scriptures and the teaching of the Church. Genuine freedom is grounded in revealed truth, not in my unbridled will. If people mistakenly try to live without any reference to any given authority they can become deeply anxious about life. It breeds a profound insecurity which can only be alleviated by encountering the love of God and surrendering to his will.

Anchored in the love of God we can make choices according to his will which significantly enrich us as human beings. A genuine Christian response will not simply adopt what I like because it makes me feel good or makes me feel unique in the world. In the love of

God we are free to be sacrificial, able to say "no" for a greater "good", and make choices aligned to what is authentically human.

The modern quest is for authenticity. In itself this is a good aspiration, but not if it means desiring to be true to myself without any accountability for my behaviour. Only in God will I find authenticity; only in him will I discover who I am and what is most important about life. Only in him will I genuinely be true to myself. Far from shackle our freedom, God liberates us from our own folly and guides us to the truth that will genuinely set us free. As Jesus said, "If you make my word your home you will indeed be my disciple and you will know the truth. And the truth will set you free" (Jn 8: 31-32).

When we pray "thy will be done on earth as it is in heaven" we fly in the face of the modern experiment. We are saying what is ultimately important is God's will, not our own. We are placing the locus of authority for our actions outside of ourselves. We acknowledge the authority of God. We are no longer claiming to be the independent, autonomous individual who will make our own life according to our own rights and desires.

To pray the Our Father is in itself an act of submission, since God's will on earth must first be done in us and by us. Our good decisions according to God's will, form good habits in us, and a life of virtue develops. In time we grow in the likeness of Jesus, showing the character of a truly godly person. Human beings can only realise their full potential through obedience to God's will; otherwise we live a self-centred, rebellious life which demeans our humanity and leads to destruction. The only way to be true to our calling is to surrender our lives to God's loving plan for us. A life of faithfulness in doing his will is guaranteed to bring the reward intended for all.

A Culture of Temporary Commitments

Our modern cultural mind-set avoids real commitment. Unfortunately, while we are liable to profess commitment we do not understand its full ramifications. We place so much value on how we feel now, and what we sense is good for us now, that we are less liable to stick with any commitment through thick and thin. We find ourselves in a culture of temporary commitments. People hold back from staking their life once and for all on a particular path given them by God.

In this context we Christians can balk at total commitment to the Lord and his way for us. Once the Cross emerges in our lives we can find excuses to withdraw from our commitment and convince ourselves that it wasn't really God's will anyway. We want God to do *our* will rather than the other way around. We are deluded by our own self-sufficiency; our lives are no longer in tune with the divine plan. Like a clock that was intended by its maker to chime at a particular time, but now misses the hour, so we are no longer in synchrony with our purposeful design. Our life is dysfunctional but we don't readily recognise it.

We are all to some degree children of the so-called Enlightenment, which aimed to wilfully exalt reason, and throw off the supposed yoke of God holding us in bondage under his authority. This "domination" is felt as demeaning of our humanity. We try to take hold of the reins and make the world according to our designs, and trust science and technology to assist in this. We refuse to obey the plan of God which we believe is oppressive of the human spirit. We believe we can build a better world by our own ingenuity and insights.

This fallacious world-view has led to a loss of any real moral compass. As we discover what we can do through technological advance we feel free to do it. The biblical story of the tower of babel speaks of this sort of pride which defies the will of God and accrues all wisdom to humanity. The consequences are a whole range of ethical disasters, such as abortion, IVF, eugenics, gender selection, and euthanasia. It is a project, if uncorrected, that will destroy humanity.

The Biblical Revelation

In Deuteronomy the Lord sets two paths before us, one that leads to life and one that leads to death. We cannot sit on the fence. We must decide. To love God is to be obedient to him.

> See today I set before you life and prosperity, death and disaster. If you obey the commandments…if you love the Lord your God and follow his ways…you will live and increase, and the Lord your God will bless you…But if your heart strays, if you refuse to listen…I tell you today you will most certainly perish…I set before you life or death, blessing or curse. Choose life then, so that you and your descendants may live in the love of the Lord your God, obeying his voice, clinging to him; for in this your life consists. (Deut 30: 15-19)

The decision is for the one true God over all false gods; repudiating wealth, status, fame, power or whatever. The question is where do I put my trust? In Jeremiah we read,

> A curse on the man who puts his trust in man, who relies on things of the flesh, whose heart turns from the Lord. He is like dry scrub in the wastelands…A blessing on the man who puts his trust in the Lord, with the Lord for his hope. He is like a tree by the waterside that thrusts its roots to the stream; when the heat comes it feels no alarm, its foliage stays green; it has no worries in a year of drought, and never ceases to bear fruit. (Jer 17:5-8)

A classic story of the fruit of disobedience is found with Saul, King of Israel. In contrast to David his successor, Saul, who was originally "seized by the Holy Spirit" and anointed by God to lead the people, failed through disobedience. The biblical author sets up the comparison between the two kings. On the one hand David is praised by God as "a man after my own heart, who will carry out my will" (Acts 13:22). Even though David had many weaknesses, his heart was set upon the Lord and doing his will. At every turn David sought the Lord's mind and obeyed him. Even when he had a major lapse through lust for Bathsheba, he was quick to repent when exposed by Nathan's prophecy.

On the other hand, Saul, lacked an obedient heart. Unlike David, he was presumptuous and arrogant before God. When it came to light that Saul had disobediently held back from the Lord what was rightfully God's, trying to cover it up by offering sacrifices, Samuel, the prophet, exposed his sham: "Is the pleasure of the Lord in holocausts and sacrifices, or in obedience to the voice of God?" (1 Sam 15:22). The anointing of God was lifted from Saul. We note the glaring omission of Saul's name in the great heroes of the Old Testament listed in Hebrews (Heb: 11:32). He doesn't rate because he failed to obey. The heart of the saints is the cry of obedience: "Lord, here I am, I come to obey your will!" (Heb 10:5; cf Ps 40:7-9)

Love Comes First

If our obedience to God is motivated by fear of authority, or avoidance of possible punishment it is deficient. We need to learn the way of love. Conforming to God's law to gain his approval or that of others is poor motivation. If we are simply trying to keep our religious score card looking good, we are not truly obeying from the heart. We must first fall in love with God, and offer ourselves in response to his unconditional love. Only when we truly love God with our whole heart and soul and mind and strength do we have the undergirding power to yield wholeheartedly to his will.

Teresa of Avila, from long experience with souls, says that to give one's will over to another is the most difficult thing of all. She writes, "to say that we abandon our will to another's will seems so easy until through experience we realise that this is the hardest thing one can do if one does it as it should be done".[31] She hints here of how we can pretend to ourselves we are surrendered to God's will, but still be compromised. We can be holding back on fully giving everything; pockets of resistance in the heart can prevent us from truly doing God's will.

This explains why Teresa goes so far as to say that it is impossible to truly surrender to God's will without the gift of contemplation. As we saw in the Introduction, by contemplation she means that our wills are captive to the love of God. We have allowed him to penetrate us with his Holy Spirit in such a way that the will is empowered to do what otherwise it would resist. Only the infilling of the Holy Spirit can make it possible to do what your will would otherwise refuse. The mark of a true disciple of Jesus is obedience to the Master, but this is not possible unless it is undergirded by a more fundamental falling in love with the Master. The Holy Spirit of love wins, persuades and overcomes our stubborn wills, igniting a fire of love which enables us to give all to Him.

Jesus our Model

Obedience is the way to God's heart. Disobedience means the loss of God. When we fall in love with God we will *want* to be obedient. Jesus makes it clear that his friends are those who do what he commands (Jn 15:14). Being obedient to God is a sign of our union with him. We can only come into friendship with Jesus by the Holy Spirit and the more we obey him the more he gives us his Spirit (Acts 5:32). We can only become obedient because Jesus has shown us the way and given us the means to do so.

We were born into solidarity with Adam, bearing the wound of the original sin, an act of disobedience that caused humanity to fall. Consequently, even after baptism, our wills are weak and prone to rebellion. Thanks be to God for the indwelling of the Holy Spirit who strengthens the will and makes it possible for us to submit gladly to God's will. Even so, Paul admits, "I find myself doing the very thing I hate" (Rom 7:19). The interior struggle to conform to God's will is not easy. Thanks be to God for Jesus Christ, who has redeemed us through a perfect act of obedience on the Cross that we were unable to make. On our behalf, in solidarity with our weak humanity, he surrendered to the Father's will.

Jesus' whole life on earth was simply doing the Father's will. At Jacob's well, when the disciples returned and found Jesus had not eaten, they expressed concern. He replied, "My food is to do the will of the one who sent me" (Jn 4:34). Elsewhere he says, "I always do what pleases him" (Jn 8.29). This expresses the existential reality of Jesus. His oneness with the Father's will is the foundation of his life. Unity of his will with the Father's will is the core of his very being. The drama of his passion was not so much about the physical agony of Roman crucifixion, but rather his interior yielding to the Father's will on our behalf.

In the Garden of Gethsemane, while sweating drops like blood, Jesus cried out, "My Father, if it is possible, let this cup pass me by. Nevertheless, let it be as you, not I, would have it" (Mt 26:39). This is the human "yes" to the Father's will that brought salvation and opened heaven's door for us. On the Cross in utter desolation he did not fall into despair but put his ultimate trust in the Father's love, dying with words of surrender on his lips, "Father, into your hands I commend my spirit" (Lk 23:46). This is what won our redemption. As Paul says, "As through one man's disobedience many were made sinners, so through one man's obedience many will be made righteous" (Rom 5:19).

We can now join our lives to that of Jesus. In Jesus and through Jesus the Father's will is wholly done. Our surrender is made possible because of his. Due to his obedience to the Father we can obey. We can overcome our self-will, autonomy and self-sufficiency. Now in Christ we can surrender to the Father's will and do what he wants. By the grace of God our human wills can embrace unreservedly God's will for our lives. The inertia of our own will constantly draws us away from the Father's will keeping us self-contained and focussed on earthly things. Praying this third petition of the Our Father we are asking for the grace to come closer to Jesus, to be drawn into his heart, so that we can conquer our self-centredness and be conformed to the Father's will.

Example of the Saints

I could choose any saint to illustrate this point. Doing the will of God is what makes a saint. But I thought to offer Charles de Foucauld to represent the "great cloud of witnesses" who in an extraordinary way have abandoned their lives to God.[32] He is a relatively recent witness and inspiring in his radical response to the Lord's love. Charles had a tortured childhood, losing both his mother and father at the age of six, he grew up under care of relatives but with lack of parenting.

Although benefiting from belonging to an aristocratic family, growing into his teenage years he was lost without any moorings. Resenting the strict discipline of a Jesuit boarding school, his faith died and he sought to compensate for his inner pain through pleasures of the flesh which never really satisfied. After attending military school he ended up in Algeria with the French foreign legion. He soon gained a reputation for wild parties, over indulging in food and drink, and maintaining a mistress on the side. His life-style was too indolent and audacious even for the army. They sacked him. Somewhat coming to his senses, he set out to explore Morocco under disguise and do what no one else had ever dared to do: an exploration and reconnaissance of Morocco, chartering its topography, geographical features, and political systems.

His report on Morocco made him famous. But now something else was happening within Charles. He could not deny the excessive fervour of the Muslim people he had encountered in North Africa. It caused him to question. Does God exist after all? He had been changed by the challenges of Africa. Now no more parties, women, and fine dinners. That all seemed useless profligacy. He was on a higher quest, but did not know where it would take him. Back in France he was seeking answers to the deeper questions. His close friend Marie de Bondy suggested talking with a priest name Abbe Huvelin who was well known for his wisdom and spiritual guidance. Charles decided he would approach this holy man. On the morning he chose to do so he found the priest waiting to hear confessions before Mass. Noticing there were no penitents Charles entered the confessional, leaned forward without kneeling, and told Abbe Huvelin he did not believe but had some questions about the Catholic faith.

The priest asked him whether he ever had faith in the past. Charles replied he did thirteen years ago but now he couldn't subscribe to many articles of the creed. The priest must have read his soul. He told Charles he had it all wrong. The problem was his impure heart; that was why he couldn't believe. He ordered him to kneel and confess. Taken aback, Charles protested. The priest forcefully repeated his command. Without really understanding what was happening Charles obeyed. He spent a long time confessing his whole life. The priest granted absolution. Charles was filled with a deep joy and a peace he had never thought possible. The priest then ordered him to go to communion in the Mass that was about to start. In making his confession Charles had relinquished his ego, and by going to Communion he received the love of Christ himself. Charles was filled with the Holy Spirit. He said afterwards, "As soon as I came to believe God was real, I understood that I could not do otherwise than live totally only for him".[33]

Charles' life was now in the hands of the Lord. He immediately wanted to embrace the most radical way possible to serve his new Master. He wanted only to do the will of God. Under the wise spiritual direction of Abbe Huvelin, to whom Charles gave his total unconditional obedience, he was held back from doing anything precipitously. However, Charles hungered for God above all else. Finally Fr Huvelin agreed for him to fulfil his desire to seek God alone. Charles set out to join a Trappist monastery in a remote region of Syria. But after nine years in this exacting way of life Charles was still not satisfied this was fully what the Lord intended for him. With the permission of his superior he headed towards the Holy Land. He felt the call to abandon himself in a way of littleness in following Jesus in his time of obscurity before the public ministry.

Not disclosing who he was he gained a job as the gardener of a convent of the Poor Clare sisters in Nazareth close to the location where Jesus, Mary and Joseph lived. He wanted a life of abject poverty in imitation of Jesus who always sought the lowest and the last place. Gradually the sisters became aware they had a saint in the back shed where he was living in simplicity. They noticed he spent long hours in their chapel adoring Jesus in the Blessed Sacrament. After some time the Mother Superior began to persuade Charles to become a priest. He resisted. His whole quest was to be the least, the most insignificant, the last in the line. However, with the help of Abbe Huvelin she prevailed.

Having been ordained, the African Sahara remained Charles' fascination. The Holy Land had been his retreat. Now his mission lay ahead. The Master was calling him. After much prayer Charles chose Beni Abbes in southern Algeria near the Moroccan border, "not knowing any more lost, abandoned and deserted country than the Sahara and Morocco".[34] There and in another place deeper into the desert he established two little fortress-like hermitages. This was a life of self-abandonment. Alone with the Lord in the wilderness, far from the comforts of European life, he devoted himself to prayer before the Blessed Sacrament as a silent witness of the good news of Jesus, and to love his Muslim neighbours by being one of them and caring for their needs. They soon recognised and respected him as a holy man.

Charles lived for his Beloved and was ready to die for him. While in Nazareth he had meditated on being a martyr, "Think that you are to die a martyr, stripped of everything, stretched out on the ground naked, unrecognizable, covered with blood and wounds, violently and painfully killed, and desire that it be today!"[35] His moment came when a band of armed men captured him outside of his hermitage. Intending to use him for ransom money, they were unexpectedly interrupted and Charles was shot through the head, then hastily buried in a shallow grave. His amazing life could be summed up by his now famous prayer of surrender:[36]

> My Father,
> I abandon myself to you.
>
> Whatever you make of me,
> I thank you.
> I am ready for everything,
> I accept everything.
>
> Provided that your will be done in me,
> In all your creatures,
> I desire nothing else Lord.
>
> I put my soul into your hands,
> I give it to you, Lord,
> With all the love of my heart,
> Because I love you,
> And because it is for me a need of love,
> To give myself,
> To put myself in your hands unreservedly,
> With infinite trust
> For you are my Father.

Call to Holiness

The greatest glory we can give to God is to do his will in everything. St Teresa of Avila says, "The whole aim of those who undertake prayer – and do not forget this, for it is very important – must be to labour and resolve and dispose oneself with all diligence he can to make one's will conform to the will of God…be very sure that in this consists all the greatest perfection which can be attained on the spiritual path".[37] The saints who have shown us what it means to imitate Jesus insist that conformity of our will to God's will is the heart of sanctity. We are to seek to do the will of God on earth as the saints do in heaven. We must call upon the Holy Spirit to empower us. As the Pentecost Sequence prays, "Bend the stubborn heart and will; melt the frozen, warm the chill". Our self-will is stubborn and resists losing its autonomy. But the Holy Spirit gives the grace to respond to the Lord with love such that we yield our will to him, and unite ourselves with his will.

An obedient heart reverences the Word of God and seeks to do it. We find the revealed will of God in the Word of Scripture, and the Church's Tradition and Magisterium. Obedience means being docile to this teaching. The Greek word used for "obedience" in the New Testament is *hupakouein*, which means to "listen under". This calls for a kind of docility whereby we are so persuaded by the truth of what we hear that we will subject ourselves to it and come under its authority. In Latin, the verb to obey is derived from *ob-audire*, which means to hearken attentively, to listen carefully. We do not read the Word of God in Scripture to dominate and control it by our clever analysis. Rather we sit under the Word, allowing it to interpret us, ready to listen to it, submit to it, and obey. We do not select some Church doctrines for our obedience and ignore or reject others. A submissive heart places oneself under the Church's authority and allows the Holy Spirit to enlighten us to the truth of her teaching. Jesus promised, "When the Spirit of truth comes he will lead you to complete truth" (Jn 16:12).

An obedient heart will also seek to discern the direction God is calling one to go. We are to be obedient to the many ways he calls. This could be for a state of life vocation to marriage, consecrated life or priesthood. We are to listen to the movements of the heart, seek advice of wise counsel, weigh up the options with a surrendered heart and desire only what God wants. Even when making lesser decisions it is important to consult the Lord first. Like Moses in the desert, who would go out daily to the Tent of Meeting to consult the Lord on when and where to go next, we need to lay our lives before the Lord, waiting upon his prompting. We are to be attentive to the quiet voice of the Shepherd within as he calls forth his sheep by name every morning (Jn 10:1-3).

We may not always get a direct answer from the Lord. But what matters is that we have invited the Lord into the discernment process and laid the matter before him. We empty ourselves of our own desires and wait on his leading. We want to avoid shutting the Lord out of the discernment process and make sure we give him every opportunity to intervene if he wishes. If we have a listening heart and have given the matter over to the Lord with genuine indifference to the outcome we can be confident he will not leave us without clarity of direction. A reassuring text in this regard is found in Isaiah: "I am the Lord unrivalled, I have not spoken in secret in some dark place. I have not said to Jacob's descendants 'seek me in chaos'. I, the Lord, speak with directness. I express myself with clarity" (Is 45:19).

A True Disciple

The genuine disciple of Jesus will be characterised by obedience. We may be very gifted by the Lord and do great works for the Church, but the touchstone of authenticity will be obedience to God's Word and submission to rightful authority. Jesus proclaimed, "It is not those who say to me, 'Lord, Lord' who will enter the kingdom of heaven, but the person who does the will of my Father in heaven". Jesus warns that exercising charismatic gifts without genuine obedience will lead to ruin: "When the day comes many will say to me, 'Lord, Lord, did we not prophesy in your name, cast out demons in your name, work many miracles in your name?" But he will say to them he does not recognise them! Why? Due to failure to obey. He explains, "everyone who listens to these words of mine and acts on them will be like a sensible man who built his house on rock. Rain came down, floods rose, gales blew and hurled themselves against the house, and it did not fall: it was founded on rock". The rock is obedience to his Word, not just listening but also *doing* the Word. Jesus makes it clear. If we are not founded on the rock of obedience we are not true disciples. We are "like a stupid man who built his house on sand. Rain came down, floods rose, gales blew and struck that house, and it fell; and what a fall it had!" (Mt 7:21-27)

Francis of Assisi once stated that "a person could give all that he has to the poor, but if he retained his self-will it would be an act of pride". We need to place our self-will on the altar with Jesus, whose will was broken before the Father for our sake, when he uttered "Father into your hands I commend my spirit". We join our wills to his self-offering on the altar that they may be broken with him, given completely to the Father for the sake of others. We cannot give anything more precious to the Lord than our will. Nothing pleases him more than to surrender our will to him, to seek to unite our will with his. We can ask the help of the Blessed Virgin Mary who perfectly embraced God's will. We cannot be more pleasing to God than when we say, "Here I am, I come to do your will" (cf. Ps 40:7-9).

The Voice of Conscience

A recent film entitled *A Hidden Life* featured the heroic story of Franz Jaegerstaetter, an Austrian farmer, who refused enlistment in the Nazi regime's army, preferring possible death to disobeying the voice of God in his conscience. Priests and his local bishop urged him not to resist, arguing his refusal would make little difference to the Nazi war machine. He adamantly held firm to his position. His agonising struggle was the consequences for his family; his death would leave his wife and three children abandoned and in danger. But his conscience would not allow him to connive in any way with a system which he knew was intrinsically evil. Franz even refused the softer option of taking a non-combatant role, since any cooperation with the war meant he would have to take the oath of allegiance to Hitler. This he could not do. He could see with clarity that the Church in Austria was compromised, yet he never criticised anyone. He simply stood on the truth as his conscience informed him.

Writing from prison with his hands in chains he said, "In a prison, no chains, not even a sentence of death, can rob a man of the faith and his own free will. God gives so much strength that it is possible to bear any suffering, a strength far stronger than all the might of the world. The power of God cannot be overcome".[38] With love in his heart for his enemies Franz stood firm in opposition to all the Nazis represented. After a prolonged imprisonment he was summonsed to a mock trial in Berlin in August 1943 at which he was condemned to death by beheading. In a letter written to his wife and mother just prior to his death, after asking their forgiveness for any way he had hurt them over the years, he continued,

> It was not possible for me to free you from the pain that you must now suffer on my account. How hard it must have been for our dear Saviour when, through his sufferings and death, he had to prepare such a great sorrow for his Mother, and they bore all of this out of love for sinners.[39]

Franz was beatified in 2007 in the Cathedral at Vienna, authorised by Pope Benedict XVI. His stance taken deliberately and peacefully, with full knowledge of the consequences, was declared a martyr's death in union with Christ crucified. In the horrible darkness of those times, Franz's moral stance was a light that could not be overcome. Even though he was told again and again by priests, bishops, and Nazi interrogators that his position would have no impact on Nazi supremacy, nor any influence on consequent history, his heart was listening to a higher voice and set upon an eternal kingdom. Only years later has this "hidden life" become a font of grace and inspiration for millions.

The Grace of Surrender

When we pray "thy will be done on earth" we are not only praying that we obey God's direct will. We are also surrendering to the *permissive* will of God. By this I mean all those circumstances out of our control that indicate the contingency of our state and our utter dependency on the Lord. We learn to embrace the will of God in all things that happen, whether in prosperity or in adversity. We gain a grace to abandon ourselves to the will of God in suffering.

Everything that happens is a means towards holiness. Paul assures us, "All things work towards the good for those who love the Lord" (Rom 8:28). And St Augustine tells us that Almighty God, because he is infinitely good, would not allow evil to exist "if he were not so all-powerful and good as to cause good to emerge from the evil itself".[40] Any suffering that comes upon us has been allowed by the Lord for a greater purpose. In the midst of adversity we cannot always see clearly, but the benefit of hindsight often shows us this truth. Rather than rail against unexpected calamities we can, after working through the initial shock, come to a place of peace and surrender, seeing that in a mysterious way this testing has come from the hand of the Lord.

Teresa of Avila, commenting on this petition, reminds us that the Lord allows suffering to come into the lives of those who love him, since he sees the courage they have. She says their love will increase as they endure their struggle:

> He will see that whoever loves him much will be able to suffer much for him; whoever loves him little will be capable of little. I myself hold that the measure for being able to bear a large or small cross is love.[41]

We can confidently place ourselves in the loving care of the Lord no matter how dire the circumstances. "Cast all your cares on him for he is looking after you" (1Pet 5:7). Through the unexpected shattering experiences that life brings we can experience the truth of his goodness and love for us. Even the most painful disappointment or the most heart-rending tragedy can become a source of grace for us. In these times of sorrow it is good to ask "Where is God in this?" He surely is there but it may take time to find his presence. At these times of trial we are invited to make a deeper "yes" to the Lord, joining with him on the Cross, sharing in the darkness of his suffering, and making his prayer our own, "Father, into your hands I commend my spirit".

The Lord never allows trials and testings to happen without giving us the interior resources to interpret them by faith, and to turn them into moments of grace. When we lose a loved one, or lose our home through accidental fire, or lose our business through economic downturn, or suffer separation or divorce, many emotions surface, and for a while the turmoil can leave us feeling devastated. But then by the grace of God, over time, we can find a new resilience to move through the pain by embracing the Cross of Jesus and surrender more deeply to the Father's will. John of the Cross reminds us,

> Remember always that everything that happens to you, whether prosperous or adverse, comes from God, so that you neither become puffed up in prosperity nor discouraged in adversity.[42]

Through suffering the Father is training us to become more surrendered to his will. "Suffering is part of our training; God is treating you as his sons. Has there ever been any son whose father did not train him?" (Heb 12:6-7). What does this mean? Through suffering we learn that nothing created can become a god for us. We are thrown upon the Lord in a new way, discovering that everything depends on him. Everything else may fail us, but God will never fail us. Even in life's greatest tragedies God will bring good out of evil, life out of death. As Paul says, "These are the trials through which we triumph, by the power of him who loved us" (Rom 8:37). The temptation during suffering is to rail angrily against God, but the man or woman of faith will be able to affirm in the midst of the worst adversity the truth that God is "just in all his ways and loving in all his deeds" (Ps 145:17). The example of Job who was tested almost to breaking point is instructive. After multiple calamities, losing all possessions and family members, his response was, "Naked I came from my mother's womb, naked I shall return. The Lord gave, the Lord has taken away. Blessed be the name of the Lord!... If we take happiness from God's hand, must we not take sorrow too?" (Job 1:21;2:10)

In suffering, as we surrender to the gentle but firm hand of the Lord, we become supple to his touch, pliable like clay in the hands of a potter (Jer 18:1-4). It can hurt when the divine potter strikes the clay with a strong blow. But the purpose is good; the emerging pot needs reshaping. He has our best interest in mind.

To change the image, suffering is a way the Lord prunes us. The divine vine dresser has to cut back the vine quite severely sometimes in order for it to grow well and bear good fruit. Jesus says "every branch that does bear fruit he (the Father) prunes to make it bear even more" (Jn 15:2). The Lord uses suffering to train our hearts to be more dependent on him. He never makes a mistake in the way he relates to us, even though we may kick and scream and resist his ways. He is always caring for us; concerned totally for our welfare. He is training us to be more surrendered to his will. As it says in Proverbs: "Like flowing water is the heart of the king in the hand of the Lord, who turns it where he pleases" (Prov 21:1). Our wills can be hard, obstinate and resistant to his work. Through suffering we are purified and refined so our hearts become more sensitive to his leading, and he can turn us where he pleases.

Abandonment to God's Will

Walter Ciszek, a Jesuit priest, ordained in 1937, is a powerful witness of what it means to surrender to God's will.[43] During his days in the Seminary he felt a compelling call to bring the good news of God's love to the Russian people. Convinced of this particular vocation, Walter trained in a centre in Rome designed to prepare future clerics for the Russian mission. However, at the time of his ordination it was impossible for priests to enter Russia. So he was appointed to a Jesuit parish in Poland. But two years later the Red Army occupied eastern Poland. He suddenly found himself able to travel into Russia with Polish refugees. Almost immediately he was arrested and spent five years in the notorious Lubianka prison for interrogation as a "Vatican spy".

Having a strong character, psychological stability and robust health he at first was able to endure the harsh conditions of solitary confinement and resist the relentless interrogations. But after countless sessions his initial optimism and self-confidence gave way to resentment and repugnance. Soon he fell into depression and just wanted to give up. After twelve months of hammering by the interrogator his mental anguish was so intense that, against his better judgement, under the threat of execution, he signed documents admitting he was a Vatican spy. Shaken and defeated, and full of self-reproach, Walter fell into despair. He blamed himself for his weakness in failing to stand firm under pressure, but he also reproached God who seemed to have abandoned him. He was racked with shame and guilt for having, under the threat of death, succumbed to the interrogator's will.

As he writhed in his misery in his lonely cell, he eventually turned to the Lord in heartfelt prayer. Walter realised that through the whole process he had been relying on himself and his own will power to withstand the interrogator's manipulations. He had failed miserably. He felt like Peter after denying the Lord. Similar to Peter he had that prideful bravado; "even if all others desert you, Lord; I will never desert you!"(Mt 26:33) Just like Peter he needed to discover that everything depends on trusting in God, not in our own strength. He realised there was too much "self" in his following of the Lord. This failure was an invitation to a new surrender to the Lord's will.

Sentenced to 15 years of hard labour in Siberia, Walter was looking forward to leaving Lubianka. But instead he was subjected to another four years of "softening up" by interrogators aiming to recruit him as a Soviet spy in the Vatican. The temptation was real. But now Walter was drawing upon a higher power than his own. He found his strength in meditating upon Jesus in the Garden of Gethsemane. Jesus sweated blood in mental anguish in anticipation of what lay before him the next day. He cried out to the Father, "Take this cup from me!" but then, "your will not mine be done". Now Walter was fully convinced that no matter what comes his way, God will be there to carry him through it. Now he was willing to make a complete gift of himself to the Lord. He wrote, "I knew I could no longer trust myself, and it seemed only sensible then to trust totally in God".[44] Under the inspiration of God's grace he recounts, "I chose, consciously and willingly, to abandon myself to God's will, to let go completely of every last reservation".[45]

Walter had found the "way through", which is the way for all genuine disciples, but a way not often taken. He began to see each day as gift bestowed by God within the confines of which we can accomplish his will. "For me each day was a series of moments and incidents to be offered back to God, to be consecrated and returned in total dedication to his will".[46] With this disposition to accept God's will every moment came a deep peace and joy he had not previously known. His newly found confidence was not in his own ability to survive, but "a total trust and confidence in God's ability to sustain me and provide me with whatever strength I needed to meet the challenges he would send me".[47]

This new attitude of total trust in God was put to the test when many sessions later the interrogator finally gave him an ultimatum to sign up as Soviet spy or face a firing squad. This time Walter happily refused to sign, ready for death, if it was God's will. Thanks be to God the threat was empty, and Walter found himself on a train to Siberia, where he laboured in the mines for another fifteen years before his release from imprisonment. His story in the labour camps involves hunger, squalor, exhaustion, death threats, prison riots, repression and extreme brutality of the guards. It is also a story of light in the darkness as he ministered the Eucharist, listened to the woes of fellow prisoners, heard their confessions, and gave them the consolation of the faith. All of this was the unfolding of a new way to live – utter abandonment to the will of God in every circumstance. When he was finally repatriated to the United States after 23 years of captivity, as part of a prisoner swap between President Kennedy and Khrushchev, people found it hard to understand how he had survived. His answer was simple: trust in the providence of God.

As it is in Heaven

The essence of heaven can be described as "where God's will is unswervingly done". Or put another way, where God's will is done, there is heaven. This petition is really another way of asking the Father, "thy kingdom come". We are praying that as God's reign takes hold in our hearts, his will be done, and earth becomes "heaven". But as mentioned earlier this prayer is not only for ourselves, but for all men and women. It has an intrinsic evangelical thrust. Immediately after Jesus gave his self-definition, that his food was to do the will of the Father, he looked up and saw the people of the town approaching. They had heard from the Samaritan woman the proclamation that he could be the Messiah, "Come and see a man who has told me everything I ever did; I wonder if he is the Christ?" (Jn 4:29) Seeing the people coming, and drawing a comparison with the crops nearby, Jesus says, "Look around you, look at the fields; already they are white for the harvest". His focus was on the salvation of all. This is why he was labouring; this is what impelled him forward; that all men and women will come to find eternal life through him. This is God's will, and we pray it may happen in our day.

For those of us who have been drawn by the Father to Jesus, there is a wonderful assurance.

All that the Father gives to me comes to me, and whoever comes to me I shall not turn away; because I have come from heaven not to do my own will, but to do the will of the one who sent me. Now the will of the one who sent me is that I should lose nothing of all that he has given to me, and that I shall raise it up on the last day. (Jn 6: 37-39)

May his will be done!

GIVE US THIS DAY OUR DAILY BREAD

Up until now we have been reflecting on the "thou" petitions, which we address to our loving Father, asking for his name to be held holy, his kingdom to come, and his will to be done on earth as it is in heaven. Now we come to the first of the four "we" petitions, asking for ourselves; that our needs here and now be fulfilled. We turn to the Father of all goodness who Jesus says gives generously to his children more than earthly fathers:

> Ask and you will receive, seek and you will find, knock and the door will be opened to you. What father among you, if his son asked for bread would give him a stone? Or if he asked for a fish would give him a snake? Or if he asked for an egg would give him a scorpion? If you then who are evil know how to give your children what is good, how much more will your heavenly Father give good things to you if you ask him? (Mt: 9-11)

In this petition we are giving voice to our implicit trust in the Father, who in his generosity and goodness will always care for our every need. We affirm again faith in the Father who always hears the cry of the poor, and who gives to all creatures "their food in due season" (Ps 104:27). He is the Father who feeds the birds of the air, and robes the flowers in the field in beauty. If he cares for these, how much more does he care for his very own children (Lk 13:24). We have no need to worry about provision; all is in the hands of our loving Father. Not one sparrow that falls to the ground is forgotten in God's sight. "Why every hair on your head has been counted. There is no need to be afraid: you are worth more than hundreds of sparrows" (Lk 12:6-7). We confidently rely upon him to care for all our material and spiritual needs. Jesus said, "Unless you become as a little child you shall not enter the kingdom of God" (Mt 18:3). With child-like trust we place our lives, our loved ones, our community and the whole of humanity in his hands.

Give Us

Our trust in God is not passive. We actively pray, "Give us". The Father loves us to ask. James says, "Why you don't have what you want is because you don't pray for it; and when you do pray and don't get it, it is because you have not prayed properly, you have prayed for something to indulge your own desires" (James 4:3). Our loving Father waits for us to show our dependence upon him. Jesus promised, "anything you ask for from the Father he will grant in my name" (Jn 16:23); that is anything that is not self-indulgent or in some way leading towards evil. When we ask with confidence and perseverance in the name of Jesus, the Father will grant it. Jesus told two parables about persistence in asking; obviously because we tend to give up too easily.

Jesus first instructs us to imagine an unexpected friend arriving, and you have no bread to offer. It is late at night, but you go to rouse your neighbour to get some bread. The neighbour refuses to get up and help. Jesus says, "I tell you, if the man does not get up and give it to him for friendship sake, persistence will be enough to make him get up and give his friend all he wants" (Lk 11:8). The key is perseverance.

Likewise, he tells of the unscrupulous judge who would not listen to a widow's plea for justice. If she keeps pleading persistently he will eventually give in, saying to himself, "I must give this widow her just rights or she will keep pestering me to death" (Lk 18:4-5). That is how we are to be with our Father! We must, as it were, "pester him to death"! Jesus comments, "Now will not God see justice done to his chosen who cry to him day and night even when he delays to help them? I promise you, he will see justice done speedily." Then Jesus finishes with the real question, "But when the Son of Man comes, will he find any faith on the earth?" Persevering faith is what matters.

The question arises: why does the Father sometimes delay in answering our prayer of petition? St Augustine suggests that the Father wants our hearts to be enlarged through the asking; we become more open to receive his grace and utterly dependent on him in a child-like way. He also says the Father does not want to treat us like spoilt children, getting everything we request immediately. That would lead to lack of gratitude, sinful presumption, and a prideful sense of entitlement.

Another way to explain the delay is that we cannot see the progression of time like God can. We can only experience time moment by moment, day by day. We may be convinced that something is right for us today, but we do not know whether it will be right for us in the future. Whereas God possesses the whole of time. When he does not answer our prayer in the present we must trust he has our best interest at heart. All time is in his hands, and all things are under his control. We simply trust him, while persisting in asking, waiting upon his good pleasure.

A Prayer of Solidarity

We saw earlier how Jesus teaches us to pray "*Our* Father"; and here in this petition to ask for "*our*" bread. Jesus invites us to pray for our needs within the communion of the disciples. We are the people who belong to God, and he has covenanted himself to us. No one is allowed to think only of oneself. We belong to brothers and sisters in Christ, and this communal dimension must never be abandoned. That is why, in the early Church, the offertory procession during the Eucharist always included gifts for the poorest and weakest in the community. The orphans and widows, the sick and disabled, prisoners and immigrants, benefited from the "bread" received as providence from the wealthy and was shared generously to those in need.[48] Their prayer to the Father requesting provision for all was not empty words but a lived reality.

But this other-centred attitude is not only in reference to the Church gathered, but also to the whole of humanity. It is a profound expression of solidarity with every person on the face of the earth. Those who have more than they need are called to share with the poor. When we pray the Lord's Prayer our hearts are open to all those who are literally hungry for "bread", for daily sustenance. The drama of widespread hunger in the world calls us to pray sincerely for provision, and to share our goods with our brothers and sisters in the human family. We are committing ourselves to take responsibility through changing our own way of life; acting in solidarity with all those who are deprived of the basics of food, clothing and shelter.

Praying for "*our* daily bread" means we cannot ignore the Lazarus at our door (Lk 16:19-20). While enjoying a relatively privileged and well-endowed way of life, we cannot block our ears to the cry of the poor. We have echoing in our hearts the words of Jesus: "I was hungry and you gave me to eat…as often as you did to the least of my brethren you did it to me" (Mt 25:35-40). If we invoke the Our Father during the Lord's Supper we cannot absolve ourselves from our fundamental commitment to help all men and women, our brothers and sisters, to obtain their daily bread. We will always hear in our hearts the words of Jesus to his disciples, "Give them something to eat yourselves" (Mk 6:37).

Trust in Providence

The Our Father is the prayer of all disciples of Jesus, who radically depend upon the Father for daily provision. "Blessed are the poor in spirit, theirs is the kingdom of heaven" (Mt 5:3). This attitude of poverty brings the blessing. The disciple may have a regular income, life savings, and superannuation benefits, together with house and land, a wardrobe of clothes, and other material comforts. But to be genuine in following Jesus, every disciple must realize all we possess is sheer gift from the Father. We are to live in gratitude for this gift and continue to be dependent on the Father for our provision. We are not to be anxious about our life and what we are to eat, what we are to wear, or where we are to live (Lk 12:29). We can be confident that these necessities will be provided. Nor are we to become inordinately attached to the gifts bestowed on us, seeking wealth or possessions for their own sake. Cultivating a detachment of heart from all material things is a mark of the genuine disciple (Lk 14:33).

Cyprian points out that the request for bread "this day" has an urgency about it. No doubt the prayer originates from the radical way the first disciples with Jesus travelled around Galilee and on the road to Jerusalem[49]. The disciples had left everything to follow Jesus. With Jesus they were radically dependent on God each day for their bread to eat, and for everything else they needed to live. From the lips of Jesus these words meant a confident appeal to the Father for food right now so he and the disciples would not starve. Jesus had told his disciples not to worry about tomorrow; they were to pray for the necessities of life for today alone. This prayer presupposes the material poverty of the disciples with Jesus. It speaks of how they renounced the splendour and riches of the world for the sake of the kingdom of God. They joyfully trusted in the Father for everything.

Luke's version of the prayer strengthens this perspective when instead of "today" Jesus says "each day", which suggests praying day by day for our basic needs. There's no presumption, but simply faith they will receive each day the food they need. He says, "Seek first the kingdom of God and his righteousness and all these other things will be given to you" (Mt 6:31). Cyprian comments:

> To those who seek the kingdom of God and his righteousness, he has promised to give all else besides. Since everything indeed belongs to God, he who possesses God wants for nothing, if he himself is not found wanting before God.[50]

This is why in the history of the Church, again and again renewal movements arise which emphasise radical evangelical poverty in imitation of Jesus and his first disciples. The early desert fathers, led by Anthony of Egypt come to mind. The first Franciscans also arose as one of the more radical examples of this recurring thrust. Historically the call to poverty in religious life has sprung out of this evangelical aspiration. I have experienced something of that impulse in my own journey and the emergence of the Missionaries of God's Love. The Holy Spirit is always making us restless and unsatisfied with our journey of discipleship. No matter what way of life one is called to follow, there will always be an unsettling sense that we have become compromised due to our love for the world, and feel a need to shake ourselves again.

Apathy and indifference towards the love of God, and towards the poor, settles too easily in the heart, and we lose our evangelical edge. This is the recurrent story of the Church in every age. In light of this propensity to compromise the gospel, the Holy Spirit will in every age raise up new movements with a desire to imitate Jesus as radically as possible. These well-intentioned movements can go astray in their enthusiastic, ascetical extremes, becoming elitist, anti-clerical, and damnatory of the Church. However, many of these movements, such as the early Franciscans and Dominicans in the thirteenth century, have been an inspiration to the whole Church and a reminder of the challenging call of the gospel not to cling tightly to anything in this world, since this earthly pilgrimage is brief, and we look forward to our homeland in heaven.

The Bread of Life

As we have seen with Cyprian, the Fathers of the Church had no hesitation to identify this fourth petition of the Our Father as a Eucharistic petition. The Our Father is prayed at the Eucharistic table prior to Communion, just as we ordinarily pray a "grace before meals". The meaning of praying for the poor mentioned earlier is not removed. It is still a prayer for the poor of the community and for alleviation of world hunger. But it also has the more spiritual meaning of expressing our hunger for Christ himself, who is the Bread of Life. The prayer still includes a cry for our daily sustenance in an earthly and practical way. But the invocation of the Father at the heart of Christian life yearns for the Bread of Life himself, who sustains us spiritually. St Cyprian, while interpreting the "bread" to be our ordinary needs of food and drink, also offers this more profound spiritual meaning. He says, "we call it our bread because Christ is the bread of those who are in union with his Body. And we ask that this bread should be given to us daily, so that we who are in Christ, and daily receive the Eucharist for the food of salvation, may not… be separated from Christ's Body".[51] By eating the Body of Christ in the Eucharist we are cleansed, purified and transformed individually, but also built more securely into the Body of Christ communally. By eating the Eucharistic Body of Christ we become more the Body of Christ.

St Augustine also has both a "material" and "spiritual" interpretation of what is meant by "daily bread". The petition, he says, involves both our daily material needs and our daily spiritual bread. However, Augustine clarifies that the spiritual bread is also the Word of God. Interpreting John 6 accurately, he insists that the Bread of Life who sustains us daily and prepares us for eternity is both the Word of God and the Eucharist: "We are praying for the needful daily bread for the body, and the consecrated visible Bread, and the invisible bread of the Word of God".[52]

The Bread of the Word

In John's gospel chapter 6 Jesus had fed the five thousand on the hillside of the lake of Galilee. He does not send them away without the necessary food. In that material sense he feeds them with bread for the day. But he does not stop there. He begins to speak about our spiritual "daily bread", which is firstly the Word of God. This is the real food we hunger for most. The Synoptic writers had already recognised this. Tempted by Satan in the desert to rely on earthly satisfaction Jesus says, "Man does not live on bread alone but on every word that comes from the mouth of God" (Mt 4:4; Deut 8:3).

Jesus rebukes the crowds that follow him after the miraculous feeding: "you are not looking for me because you have seen the signs but because you have had all you wanted to eat" (Jn 6:26). We do not live on material bread alone. We need his Word, which cannot be divorced from who he is, the Word of Life. The eternal Word has become bread for us by taking flesh and now speaks to us in human words, which come from God. Jesus proclaims he is the bread of life come down from heaven. Anyone who comes to him will never be hungry; the one who believes in him will never thirst (Jn 6:35).

His Word will satisfy the deepest hunger of the soul. What is this hunger? It is the hunger for fullness of life, rather than an aimless life without meaning or purpose. To receive his words and respond with faith brings eternal life. "Yes it is the Father's will that whoever sees the Son and believes in him shall have eternal life, and that I shall raise him up on the last day" (Jn 6:40). It's a hunger to be able to make sense of our world and all of the suffering and seeming absurdity of life. We want meaning that will light up our minds and hearts, show us the way in the darkness of a secularised world, and give peace to souls.

When people began to walk away from Jesus, he turned to his disciples asking whether they will also go. Peter answered, "Lord to whom shall we go; you have the words of eternal life" (Jn 6:67). Here Peter attests to his dependency on the daily words of Jesus. The Greek here is not "*logos*" as expected, but "*rhema*", meaning the daily word for the moment, the word that speaks to the heart now and provides light in the darkness, hope in the storm and wisdom for the way ahead. There is a famine on earth "not a famine of bread, nor a thirst for water, but of hearing the words of the Lord" (Am 8:11). It is most profoundly a hunger for love, to really know God's love for us revealed in the word of Jesus, and it is a hunger for a new capacity to love and be loved by others. This petition not only asks that we would ourselves be fed on the Word of God, but that we as Church would take up the proclamation of the Word ever more faithfully. It is God's will that this deepest hunger of the human soul be satisfied.

The Bread of the Eucharist

The ultimate way human hunger can be satisfied is in the Eucharist. This divine food was prefigured in the manna given to the Israelites in the desert. But Jesus says to the Jews, "Your fathers ate the manna in the desert and they are dead; but this is the bread that comes down from heaven…Anyone who eats this bread will live forever". And what is this bread that brings eternal life? He continues, "the bread that I shall give is my flesh for the life of the world" (Jn 6:50-51). Our daily bread is none other than Jesus, the Word incarnate, himself. "Anyone who eats my flesh and drinks my blood has eternal life, and I shall raise him up on the last day" (Jn 6:54). Only this food can ultimately satisfy the deepest hunger in the human heart for love and for meaning.

If our need for love is not satisfied we can do crazy things, acting outside of our normal moral boundaries, often damaging ourselves and others. This deep yearning to be loved and to love can drive people into poor decisions and disastrous relationships. Ever since the fall of Adam and Eve human beings have been struggling to control the all-consuming desire to possess and to use the other for their own gain. Jesus offers himself to us as food that will ultimately satisfy our deepest craving: "I am the bread of life. Whoever comes to me will never be hungry, and whoever believes in me will never thirst" (Jn 6:35). The encounter with Jesus in the sacrament of love ministers deeply to the soul. Therese of Lisieux shares her experience of first Holy Communion as the consummation of a long-desired intimacy with Jesus:

> Ah! How sweet was the first kiss of Jesus! It was a kiss of love, I felt that I was loved, and I said: 'I love you and I give myself to you forever! There were no demands made, no struggles, no sacrifices; for a long time now Jesus and poor

little Therese had looked at and understood each other. That day it was no longer simply a look, it was a fusion; they were no longer two, Therese had vanished as a drop of water is lost in the immensity of the ocean. Jesus alone remained; He was Master, the King.[53]

In filling us with his love Jesus promises us fullness of life which brings ultimate meaning to our existence: "As I, who am sent by the living Father, draw life from the Father, so whoever eats me will draw life from me" (Jn 6:57). Jesus is saying that his reason for living is because of the Father. Likewise, when we eat of him we live because of him. Partaking of him gives ultimate purpose to one's life, providing the reason for living here on this earth, and life forever in heaven.

Daily Bread

The Eucharist is the real presence of Jesus, the bread of life, given for us now, and also the pledge of future glory with him in heaven. We have already encountered this eschatological tension between the "already" but "not yet" of the kingdom of God. The Eucharistic food is both an existential experience now of God's goodness, and also an anticipation of life with him forever. We pray "give us this day our *daily* bread". "Daily" renders the Greek word *epiousios*. This is an extremely rare and obscure word. So much so that Origen maintained that it was probably coined by the evangelists themselves. While that may be a fanciful claim, we need to draw out its significance. The word is usually translated "daily" but it could actually mean "for tomorrow". Translators differ. Some will insist on "daily bread", meaning "what is necessary for existence now" i.e. what we need in order to live. Others argue the correct translation would be "bread for the future" i.e. for the days ahead. Could this mean the "great tomorrow", the day of the second coming of the Lord when we will experience the heavenly banquet prepared for all who are faithful? I suggest it would be stretching the evidence too far to land exclusively in the latter camp. However, a more convincing possibility is to opt for the "already" but "not yet". So the petition would mean "Give us this day our bread for tomorrow". The emphasis is on what we need for today, right now, but with an eschatological dimension. We know that this Eucharistic meal, while meeting our deepest needs now, is a foretaste of a greater, more splendid banquet in the fullness of the kingdom yet to come.

In summary, we have seen that in asking the Father for our daily bread we are firstly trusting him with what is necessary for our life; that he will take care of our material needs, as long as we do not become inordinately attached to our possessions, and succumb to the economic greed of our contemporary culture. We are also begging the Father on behalf of all our brothers and sisters in the world who are physically hungry. Secondly, we are asking the Father for the bread of the word of Jesus to be fed to as many people as possible. That we ourselves would eat the words of Scripture daily, and also become evangelists and teachers, sharing this vital spiritual food with all and sundry. We want the hunger in every human heart for love and meaning to be met by the Word of God, and we want all people to open their hearts to Christ, the Word incarnate, who is the bread of life. Thirdly, we are asking the Father to continue to feed us with Christ, the Bread of Life in the Eucharist. This is for the good of our own souls bringing us into intimacy with Christ, but also so that we will be more deeply in communion with all our brothers and sisters in the Body of Christ, the Church. Through the Eucharistic bread we are made one, and saved from separation from the Body. Even when we sin and break bonds with the Body we pray for the grace of repentance and readmission into the communion of the disciples, which is our means of salvation and restoration.

FORGIVE US OUR TRESPASSES AS WE FORGIVE THOSE WHO TRESPASS AGAINST US

Beg for Mercy Upon Us

In this petition we cry out for mercy. With a contrite heart, recognising our own personal faults and failings, and our complicity with the sin of the world, we ask for forgiveness. We are all sinners. "All have sinned and fallen short of the glory of God" (Rm 3:23). Left to ourselves we cannot repair the damage done by our sin against God and against others. With the prodigal son we turn back to the Father's house to acknowledge our sin. We put our trust in the merciful Father who runs to us and throws his arms around us and kisses us tenderly. Like the tax-collector at the back of the Temple we cry out, "God, be merciful to me a sinner" (Lk 18:9-14). We do not come to the Father like the Pharisee, praying to himself, rather than to God, and making himself look good before God. We choose not to come with pretence or a social mask, parading our good deeds before him. Rather, we come in honesty, being real about our need for mercy; without God it is not possible for us to be free of our sin. Without his power we cannot break the patterns of thinking and acting which enslave us. We admit our incapacity to grow in virtue, our utter need for the redeeming power of God brought to us through the blood of Jesus poured out on the Cross. In the sacrament of Reconciliation we have a privileged moment of encounter with his abundant mercy.

Beg for Mercy on the Church

This petition is not only an individual cry to God for mercy. It is also a collective plea: "forgive *us* our trespasses". This is the Church's prayer. Together we beseech the Lord to forgive us. These days as a Church we are on our knees begging God's mercy upon us and his purifying work due to our many transgressions. In the wake of the clergy sexual abuse crisis, and the ongoing scandals in the Church, we need to approach God with honesty, not seeking to cover up our sins. After David had fallen into lust with Bathsheba he attempted to cover up his fault by arranging for her husband, Uriah, to be slain in battle. This was not pleasing to the Lord; he sent the prophet Nathan to tell him the story of a rich man in the land who had forcibly taken a poor man's only lamb for himself to feed a guest. David was inflamed with anger at this injustice. "As the Lord lives" he said to Nathan, "that man deserves to die". And Nathan said to David, "You are the man!" (2 Sam 12:1-7). The Holy Spirit will convict us in this way: "You are the one!" There is no point, as individuals or as Church, to be looking at others in the world and judging them. We must first look at our own sin and repent in earnest before God. Only then can we be an authentic prophetic voice for others.

Beg for Mercy on the Whole World

We are praying that the whole of humanity will turn back to God, like the people of Nineveh, who collectively repented when Jonah preached repentance (Jonah 3:8). At the time of writing, the COVID 19 infection is spreading rampantly throughout the world, leaving a path of devastating sickness and death. While it is too simplistic to see this as God's judgement upon us, we can certainly experience it as a sign of our need for repentance. God is shaking the foundations of our world in order to free us from things to which we have been too attached. He is calling us back to being founded in his kingdom and genuine righteousness.

We pray that the Spirit of God will move in the hearts of all men and women helping us to change our values and ways of thinking and to build a new culture of life and love according to the ways of God. As with the other petitions in the Our Father this one is all-embracing; a prayer for every man and woman, for all cultures and nations. We are beseeching God that the rebellion in hearts which began with Adam's sin will be reversed by a wide scale return to God and a readiness to welcome the redemption won for the human race in Jesus.

We are humbly asking God for forgiveness for all our sins and for all the sins of the world. We seek to have "perfect" contrition i.e. sorrow for our sins because they have offended against the infinite goodness of God. We are aware of the suffering that Jesus endured on the Cross for our sake and the price he paid for our sins. We feel this deeply and know the pain of having offended him and the distress for the way he has been offended by others. We are aware that our sins nailed him to the Cross, and are grateful for the love in his heart broken open for us from which flowed blood and water for our redemption. We turn to the Father, who in infinite compassion suffered with Jesus as he hung on the Cross, and willingly gave over his only Son for our sake.

As we Forgive Those who Trespass Against Us

To understand this second part of the petition we need to ask what the adverb "as" means. Does it mean that God will only forgive us to the extent that we forgive others? Is God's forgiveness dependent on our forgiveness? If that was the case then it would mean God waits for us to produce within ourselves the power to forgive, and only then would he be ready to forgive us. But this warped thinking forgets the primacy of God's grace. We are utterly unable to forgive anyone without the grace of God. Forgiveness is a divine gift with which we must cooperate. God has loved us first, and only because of his love are we able to love others.

The power to forgive others comes first through our personal experience of God's forgiveness. Pope Francis speaks about this often. "Only the person who feels forgiven is capable of forgiving. I forgive because first I have been forgiven". He is speaking from his own experience of forgiveness. At the age of 17 he experienced the mercy of God in the sacrament of reconciliation which changed his life.[54] After his election as Pope, reporters asked him "Who is Jorge Bergoglio?" He immediately answered, "He is a sinner, who knows the mercy of God". In that teenage experience he received forgiveness which shaped the rest of his life. It was the feast of St Matthew. Later he chose as his motto the words of Bede the Venerable about the calling of Matthew the tax collector. *"Miserando atque eligendo"* meaning "Looking upon him with mercy he called him". That is how the Pope experienced the touch of the Lord. He says he wept with joy. Looking back now when faced with the need to forgive someone he says to himself, "There's no comparison; this is a small thing compared with the time God showed me great mercy".

A debt we could not pay

Now we must look at the parable of the unforgiving servant. Jesus tells the story of a servant who owed his master ten thousand talents, the equivalent of six million dollars (Mt 18:23-35). He had no way of paying the debt and begged for time, otherwise he would be thrown into prison. The master was moved to pity and cancelled the debt outright. One would think the servant would be so grateful for such a gift. But instead he went outside, found a fellow servant who owed him 100 denarii, the equivalent of about ten dollars. He began to throttle this fellow and threaten him and his family with prison until he paid back the full amount. When the master heard about this he was angry and had the ungrateful servant thrown to the torturers. What is the message here?

We are meant to appreciate that our burden due to sins was similar to that servant. The debt we owed God because of our sins was infinitely more than 6 million dollars. It was impossible for us to pay. But God in his great mercy sent his only Son into the world to save us. On the Cross Jesus, by taking our place, cancelled the debt owing to our sins (Col 2:14). Should we not be grateful? The little offences that people make against us are nothing in comparison to what Jesus paid to free us from our sin. If we realize his mercy, and experience forgiveness of our sins, surely we should be prepared to forgive the comparative peccadillos of our brothers and sisters! We notice in the parable that even though the servant had been bestowed mercy, he had not been willing to receive it, witnessed by his ungrateful attitude and lack of mercy to his fellow servant. This explains the "as" in the petition under consideration. Unless we take hold of God's mercy and bestow mercy on others, we will lose everything.

The sign that we have really appropriated his mercy to us will be the degree to which we show mercy to others. If I hold out against my brother or sister and refuse to forgive, I forfeit the grace of God so readily given to me. If I am full of bitterness, resentment and hatred towards my brother or sister it's impossible for the gift of God's mercy to penetrate my heart. Only when I choose to forgive do I open the channel again for God's mercy to find a dwelling place within me.

We can see from the parable that if I harden my heart to another then I have hardened my heart to God. As John says, "How can you say you love God who is invisible when you do not love the brother or sister who is visible?" (1 Jn 4:20) If I choose not to have mercy on my brother or sister then I have shut myself out from the mercy of God. To refuse to open my heart to my brother or sister is to forfeit the grace of God's mercy upon me. That is why the parable says the unforgiving servant was thrown out to the torturers. The most tortured people I know are those who refuse to forgive another. They hold up a fist inside themselves against this person or this institution and will not let go. They refuse to withdraw the judgment they have on that person and will not give the judgment over to God. So they make their own prison for themselves and are tortured in their souls.

Forgiveness: a Gift of God

The 1994 violent outbreak of genocide in Rwanda unleashed a soul-numbing level of hatred and brutality, leaving hundreds of thousands of victims mercilessly hacked to death simply because they were ethnically undesirable, seen as "cockroaches" not worthy of life. Could a survivor whose whole family was slaughtered by their neighbours ever forgive? Immaculee Ilibagiza is an extraordinary witness that by the grace of God it is possible.[55] After hiding in a bathroom concealed behind a cupboard for months, Immaculee miraculously escaped death. But when the genocide ceased she had to face the devastating reality of returning to her home village to see the destruction first hand. Having a deep Catholic faith, a love for Jesus and Mary, she had wanted to forgive. She knew that was God's way and also the only way to freedom for herself. But the journey back to the village, and being confronted with the carnage firsthand, left her shattered. That night she writhed in pain finding it impossible to sleep:

> My soul was at war with itself. I'd struggled so hard to forgive but now felt duped for having done so; I had no clemency left in me. Seeing my home in ruins and visiting the lonely, forgotten graves of my loved ones had choked the life out of my forgiving spirit. When my neighbours whispered the stories of my family's sadistic murders in my ear, the feelings of hatred that I thought I'd banished from my soul sprang violently from the depths of my being with renewed vigour. My heart hungered for revenge, and I raged inside myself. Those *bloody animals!* They are *animals, animals, animals!*[56]

She could feel the weight of her negative thoughts dragging her into darkness. "I never felt lonelier that night. God was my truest friend, and these feelings were a wall between us. I knew my thoughts caused him pain, and that knowledge tortured me." She was now on her knees begging the Lord for forgiveness for the hateful thoughts, and beseeching him to fill her with the power of his love and forgiveness. She prayed in desperation, "Those who did these things are still your children, so let me help them, and help me to forgive them. O, God, help me to love them". With this prayer she experienced a rush of air in her lungs; a deep sigh of relief. She was at peace. Bitterness and hatred were dissipated. The anger that had gripped her like a cancer was gone. She says, "I asked God for the forgiveness which would end the cycle of hatred – hatred that was always dangerously close to the surface".[57]

Immaculee was able to consolidate that attitude of forgiveness over the coming months and years. The very next day she asked to be taken back to the village to give her family members a proper burial. As painful as it was, this provided some needed closure. A few weeks later she asked to be taken to the prison where the man, who was the leader of the gang responsible for the death of her mother and beloved brother was being held. They dragged into the room a dishevelled, limping old man, who she immediately recognised. She had played with his children as she was growing up in the village. He had been a respectable man and a family friend. The man was roughly thrown onto his knees in front of her. When he looked up and saw who it was, the colour drained from his face and he crouched down in fear and shame. The prison commander was abusing him, and demanding him to explain why he murdered her mother and brother. The battered man remained on the floor unable to look up and face her. He was emaciated, bruised from many bashings, his once-handsome face filthy, and sores all over his body. Immaculee was moved to compassion; she wept. She could see how he had been overtaken by the evil one, and this had ruined his life. She says, "I was overwhelmed by pity for the man". The commandant dragged the poor man to his feet demanding "What do you have to say to her?" Immaculee relates how the man was sobbing bitterly and covered with shame "He looked up at me only for a moment, but our eyes met. I reached out, touched his hands lightly, and quietly said what I'd come to say, "I forgive you".[58]

A Decision to Love

In the gospels there are a number of "as" sayings. Jesus said, "You must be perfect *as* your heavenly Father is perfect" (Mt 6:14-15). It is good to note that the Greek word "*erchomai*" is used here which means "to become" rather than "is". That's a relief, because no one is perfect until heaven. We are on the road to *becoming* perfect. The sign of how perfect we are is the degree to which we love others.

In a similar mode, Jesus said "Be merciful *as* your heavenly Father is merciful". This cannot be achieved by trying to model ourselves on Jesus through looking at his good example in showing mercy. No, it must happen from within the heart. When Christ dwells within us by the Holy Spirit this change can be effected.

I can only become like Jesus and have his merciful heart to the extent that he abides in me, and I cooperate with his grace. A genuine change of heart is necessary. Therese of Lisieux is a good witness to this. She had a natural aversion for one of the sisters in her convent[59]. She couldn't reconcile this with the command of Jesus, "love one another *as* I have loved you". In her incapacity to love she cried out to the Lord. He replied by assuring her it was possible to love, but not in her own strength. She needed to invite him more deeply into her heart and then she could love. She did so. And after making the decision to love her sister and to practically do acts of kindness for her best, Therese was able to win the battle. She knew she was celebrating the victory of Jesus won for us on the Cross, and in faith applied to her life.

We should note that this petition on forgiving others was considered so important to Matthew that it is the only petition Jesus returns to at the end of the prayer: "Yes, if you forgive others their failings, your heavenly Father will forgive you yours; but if you do not forgive others your Father will not forgive your failings either" (Mt 6:14-15). Again it is clear that God's forgiveness, which is so readily given to all whose hearts are open, cannot be received by those who have hardened their heart against another. In shutting their heart to the one they can see, they in effect shut their heart to God whom they cannot see. Obviously Matthew wanted to drive home the difficulty involved in forgiving and the need to work hard on this aspect of discipleship.

Forgiveness is a decision, not a feeling.[60] We cannot always alleviate the pain of the offence, particularly when there has been a loss of trust. But we can choose to give it over to the Lord and have compassion for the offender. This change of heart can only come from the grace of God. Nor can we easily forget what has happened. We don't have to forget. In fact it is advisable not to forget, but to have the memory purified by the grace of God. Over time we can remember the incident gracefully, and pray for the one who offended us. Again this can only come from the Holy Spirit at work within us.

Sometimes it is just not possible to be reconciled, to actually walk again in relationship with the other. But we can let go of resentment and bitterness, allow the Lord to heal the heart so that we hold no enmity for the person or seek any revenge. We can by the grace of God pray a blessing on the perpetrator. This is the only way our heart will be set free from a self-imposed prison. Otherwise, we are destined for perpetual torture. As Jesus warned in the parable, after the merciless servant was given to the torturers: "So also my heavenly Father will do to every one of you, if you do not forgive your brother from the heart" (Mt 18:35). The truth must be declared: the consequence of refusing to forgive is self-inflicted torture.

A Tortured Soul Finds Peace

In 1944 when the Nazis were driven out of France by the Allies, there were angry court cases and swift sentences against any French people who had collaborated with the German occupation.[61] One man, named Jacques, when he was drinking too much, was bragging about his bravery during the Occupation. But he dropped a loose comment that his friend Martin was a possible collaborator. Jacques was summoned for questioning about his comment. He was scared and panicked, making up stories to incriminate Martin. As a result Martin was sentenced to prison for 20 years. In 1957 Martin was given an early release. During his imprisonment his wife had died and his son was killed in the French Indo-China war. He still carried intense hatred for his friend who had given false evidence against him.

He returned to the family home which had been unoccupied and locked since his wife's death. Upon entering he found a letter that his wife had written to him just before she died. In the letter she made a dying request for Martin to go to Lourdes where they used to go on pilgrimage before the War. Martin felt obliged to fulfil his wife's dying wish. She had been the only one to stand by him all these years. On arrival in Lourdes he went down towards the Grotto, brooding over his wasted life. Surprisingly, a young woman approached him and offered him a glass of water. Startled, he nervously took the glass and drank. Then awkwardly handed it back, mumbling thanks, and walked away. As he passed the Grotto he heard a priest preaching, "Father, forgive us as we forgive others." Martin's anger flared. How dare he tell me to forgive!

For some unaccountable reason Martin began to spill out his tragic story to another priest who listened to him. The priest suggested he fulfil his wife's dying wish and go back to the Grotto which he had avoided. The girl was still there. He asked her why she had offered him a glass of water. She blushed and said apologetically, "Forgive me for seeming rude but you looked so miserable when you came down here earlier. You seemed to be so sad and burdened that I asked Our Lady to help you first before she heard my petition." Martin's curiosity was aroused. "What's your problem, what brought you here?" he asked. "My father is dying" she replied "the doctor said his heart can't last much longer. I'm not praying for his cure. But he's dying with terrible guilt, and that's why I've come to ask Our Lady to help him. After the war he betrayed a boyhood friend to one of those tribunals and the man was given a twenty year jail sentence. My father is convinced God will never forgive him because he can never undo the evil he did. I can't bear seeing him die without hope."

Martin looked at her face more closely. He gasped "Why you are Marguerite!" "How do you know me?" she asked. "Because I now remember you when you were little. I am the man your father betrayed!" She went white and turned to run. He grabbed her wrist, "Marguerite, stop! You were kind to me this morning. Now do me one more favour. I can't recite the last part of the Our Father. I think you know the part I mean. Please!" A shaken Marguerite stumbled through the prayer, helping Martin to say the words. He sighed as if a boulder had been lifted off his chest. "Thank you Marguerite. Now let us go together to see if we can't help your father."

How wonderful are the ways of God! How rich he is in mercy! What a grace-filled moment when Martin could pray the words, "Forgive us our trespasses as we forgive those who trespass against us!" What an extraordinary moment for Jacques when the man whom he betrayed now comes to bring forgiveness! He could now die in peace. The most striking feature of this story is that both the one offended and the offender were living in a hell of hatred; Martin in his hatred for his betrayer, Jacques in self-hatred for having betrayed his boyhood friend. Both encountered the mercy of God, and could pray the Our Father together. And let us not overlook that all this took place in the context of the intercession of the Blessed Virgin Mary, the Mother of mercy.

The Power of the Cross

The grace of forgiveness has been won for us by Jesus. The way to forgiveness is through the Cross of Jesus. On the Cross Jesus entered into the worst hell-like agony that has afflicted the human heart because of our sin. In solidarity with us in our human plight, he willingly entered into the consequences of the darkest, ugliest sins of humanity. Crying out "My God, my God, why have you abandoned me". But he did not despair. Being one with us, his trust and surrender to the Father turned hatred into love, evil into goodness, slavery into freedom. "For our sake God made the sinless one into sin, so we may become the righteousness of God" (2Cor 5:21).

When Jesus was being nailed to the Cross with excruciating agony wracking his whole body, he cried out "Father forgive them for they know not what they do". This heart of forgiveness has breathed new life into a world captive to sin. Jesus has forever broken the cycle of violence which keeps the world in bondage. He met violence with forgiveness; without any revenge or retaliation. His blood was shed for all. No one was excluded from his merciful heart. The savagery of human hatred and revenge died with him. Now all who are baptised into his death and resurrection can live free of resentment, finding in their heart a grace to forgive.

Grace in Tragedy

On a hot January night in 2019 in Oatlands, Sydney, two families were shattered and left with a grief beyond compare. A drunk driver's out of control utility truck mounted the curb and killed four of their children who were on their way to buy ice-creams. Leila and Danny Abdallah lost three of their children instantly; 13-year old Anthony, 12-year old Angelina, and nine-year-old Sienna. Their 11-year-old cousin Veronique Sakr was also killed. In news footage the next day Leila and Danny told reporters they were not the sort of people who hate. While they wanted the driver to face justice they chose not to live in resentment but to forgive. Thus began a painful journey for them with many despairing moments. Their strong Maronite Catholic faith sustained them through this horrific time of darkness and the agony of loss.

In a memorial event one year after the tragic deaths of their children Leila and Danny faced the press again. On the anniversary, in memory of their children they were inaugurating i4Give Day[62] as an inspiration for all those who struggle with resentment and find it difficult to forgive. Leila and Danny spoke of their journey of grief and how they found the grace to forgive the driver. They attributed this grace to their Christian faith in Jesus whose love on the Cross makes it possible for us to love when it seems beyond us to do so. Danny shared how each day there has been pain, emptiness, and tears of hopelessness: how hard it has been to celebrate birthdays. Yet they are consoled by their conviction that their children are in heaven.

He went on to say that forgiveness has helped him to get rid of the anger, resentment and bitterness: "This has allowed us to live in a state of peace and grace, and I promise you if my children were here today they'd say, 'Forgive him'". Leila shared how they had to make a decision in the heart which set them free: "We chose to turn our tragedy into a greater goodness. We chose to carry our cross with dignity. We chose forgiveness and love over hatred....Forgiveness is the greatest gift you can give yourself and to others". They chose not to hate, but to love. They chose light in the darkness. As Leila says, "Forgiveness brings healing to the hurting soul and allows you to have peace in your heart".

A Way to Pray

When we find it difficult to forgive it can be helpful to imagine ourselves at the foot of the Cross of Jesus with the person we need to forgive standing next to us. Both are totally dependent on the blood Jesus shed for us; only by his blood can we be purified of our sin. Together with the one who we find difficult to forgive we realise that it is only by the mercy of God that any of us can stand at all. "If you, O Lord, should mark our guilt who would survive? But with you is found forgiveness, for this we revere you" (Ps 130:3-4). Standing at the foot of the Cross softens the heart. His blood shed completely for each of us will cleanse us and empower us to forgive. In our shared weakness we can embrace the other from the heart.

LEAD US NOT INTO TEMPTATION

New Wording?

Pope Francis recently suggested a change of wording for this petition. He is concerned that the traditional translation implies that God induces temptation, which is contrary to his nature. The Pope explains, "I am the one who falls. It is not God pushing me into temptation". He prefers a rewording: "do not let us fall into temptation".[63] The Italian Bishops conference, wanting to avoid an incorrect image of God, have adopted this formula. The change is supported by a text in James: "When tempted, no one should say 'God is tempting me'. For God cannot be tempted by evil, nor does he tempt anyone" (James 1:13). Interestingly the ancient Syriac translation of this petition supports the Pope's change. In the Syriac, which is very close to the original Aramaic, the petition is rendered as "Do not let us fall/go into temptation". And the Syriac translation is much older than the one we have learnt as children, which originated in the English Prayer Book of 1549.

Yet the new translation is controversial, particularly because Tertullian, followed by Cyprian of Carthage in the third century, agreed with the received translation, "lead us not into temptation". But to avoid misunderstanding, they interpreted the meaning as "do not suffer us to be led into temptation". Similarly, Augustine of Hippo, in the fourth century, did not see a need to change the text. Whether a change should be made becomes merely a textual debate, since no one wants to affirm that God tempts us.

The Catholic Catechism doesn't suggest a change in the traditional words in the prayer itself, but highlights the text from James, which insists that God does not tempt anyone; rather, he wants to set us free from evil. The Catechism notes it is difficult to translate the Greek verb rendered as "lead". It offers two meanings: "do not allow us to enter into temptation" and "do not let us yield to temptation".[64] Both these renditions support Pope Francis's suggestion. So we are praying to God the Father to protect us from falling into temptation. We acknowledge our weakness, knowing that without God's help we will give in to the desires of the flesh.

Can Anything Good Come from Temptation?

While I support Pope Francis' new wording, I suggest we need to be careful not to miss something implicit in the traditional literal translation, which could be lost in the papal rendition. In the gospel we are told, "Then Jesus was led by the Spirit into the wilderness to be tempted by the devil" (Mt 4:1). Jesus was led by the Spirit into a situation where he would be severely tested by the enemy of our human nature. Clearly the temptation comes from the devil, not from God. But is there a mysterious way in which God's redemptive plan is fulfilled even through temptation? Jesus, we are told in Hebrews, "was tempted in every way we are but did not sin" (Heb 4:15). And the purpose of this was redemptive! "For because he himself has suffered and been tempted, he is able to help those who are tempted" (Heb 2:18). God the Father did not directly beset Jesus with temptations, yet he allowed them to happen. They were crucial in the redemptive plan. Through his victory over them, Jesus, in solidarity with our human weakness, made it possible for us to have victory also.

The ultimate temptation for Jesus was in the Garden of Gethsemane. After Jesus had resisted firmly the temptations in the desert, Satan left him "to return at the appointed time"; a reference to Jesus' interior agony in the Garden, when he was "sorrowful to the point of death". This most insidious temptation for Jesus was to lose trust in the Father. Instead he humbly yielded to the Father's will: "your will, not mine, be done". Then, having resisted Satan's lies, and surrendered to the Father, he proclaimed as he was arrested, "This is your hour; this is the reign of darkness" (Lk 22:53). Right up to Calvary Jesus is tested for our sake. Why? So that his "no" to Satan, and his "yes" to the Father, having total trust in him, may redeem us.

In this same vein we can see that our own path to holiness involves temptations. Testings are a necessary part of the journey for everyone. Those who are very close to the Lord undergo even more intense testing. We only have to look at the embattled figure of Antony of Egypt in the desert beset by demons, or Therese of Lisieux in an enclosed Carmelite convent tempted to despair, or Ignatius Loyola at Manresa attacked by scruples, and tempted to throw himself into a well. God allows temptations so we are purified of pride and become more totally dependent on him. This is the case not only with major saints, but also for anyone in the early stages of the spiritual journey. Temptations to indulge in a particular vice function in God's plan as a way of growing in the opposing virtue. For example, as we resist the temptation to lust we grow in chastity; as we resist the temptation to unbridled anger, we grow in gentleness, and so on. The classic text of assurance in times of battle is provided by St Paul, "God is faithful. He will not let you be tempted beyond your strength, but with every temptation he will provide the way of escape, that you may be able to endure it" (1Cor 10:13).

From these considerations we can make some sense of the traditional translation "lead us not into temptation". We are asking God not to send trials that would be beyond our capacity to resist.

We are reminding the Lord of our weakness and proneness to evil. If according to his wisdom he is going to allow temptations to come, we plead not to let them be too tough, but to remember our frailty. We also ask for his protecting hand upon us, especially when a temptation starts to become too much for us. St Cyprian interpreted the petition in this way:

> The enemy can do nothing against us unless God has allowed it beforehand, so that our fear, our devotion and our worship may be directed to God – because the Evil One is not permitted to do anything unless he is given authorisation.[65]

God sometimes grants the Evil One a limited power so that we realise how poor we are in faith and love and not presume upon his grace, or become too complacent about virtue gained. So this petition expects that we will be put to the test in our spiritual lives, but begs the Father not to allow us to falter under the pressure of the temptation, and not to fall for the lies of the Enemy that we do not have the strength to endure.

Do Not Let us Fall into Temptation

But let us return to Pope Francis' focus. This is surely the primary meaning of the petition. Firstly, we need to distinguish between temptation and sin. If we are tempted we have not yet sinned until we consent to the temptation. If we deliberately entertain the temptation and take pleasure in it, to that degree we have begun to sin. But if the will holds firm against a temptation we have not sinned. However, if we cave in under pressure and go with the temptation then we have fallen. James expresses it poignantly, "Everyone who is tempted is attracted and seduced by his own wrong desire. Then the desire conceives and gives birth to sin, and when sin is fully grown, it too has a child, and the child is death" (James 1:15).

When we earnestly ask "do not let us fall into temptation" we are simply praying that in the hour of temptation we do not fall into sin. Jesus told his disciples in the Garden that they were to stay awake and to pray not to be put to the test (Mt 26:41). This is a succinct summary of the best strategy to avoid falling into temptation: watch and pray. We don't want to be caught asleep like the apostles. Being awake and vigilant is crucial. Paul tells us the enemy attacks when we least expect. Even when we are in a time of consolation we need to be alert. The Enemy does not sleep. Neither does the Lord Jesus Christ, and all his angels and saints. Thanks be to God! But we must be alert to the battle. Daily we must put on the armour of God or we "will not be able to put up any resistance when the worst happens, or have enough resources to hold your ground" (Eph 6:13).

Vigilance of the Heart

Being vigilant means guarding the heart from the incursions of the evil one. We must be careful to bring to the light perverse thoughts or desires as soon as possible. Ignatius Loyola says the enemy acts like a false lover, seducing under cover of darkness[66]. If he is exposed he flees. One of the best protections is a commitment to bring to the light one's temptations before a spiritual director or trusted counsellor. Otherwise the desire becomes more intense and the evil one feeds you with lies; the mind becomes clouded and you are in the grip of passion that seems uncontrollable. "If we live our lives in the light, as he is in the light, we are in union with one another, and the blood of Jesus, his Son, purifies us from all sin" (1Jn 1:7).

Guarding against temptation also means daily taking time to reflect on the interior movements of the heart; what we have allowed to happen within us. We need to discern whether we have given ground to the evil one, yielding to the persuasion of the flesh, or disorder of the mind, or compromised behavioural patterns. This regular *examen* of the heart recommended by Ignatius keeps us vigilant, since most temptations arise over a period of time as we allow the heart to become divided and more prone to sin.

Being vigilant also means guarding your weakest point. The enemy is like a shrewd military commander who will hammer away with his weapons at the weakest point in the opposing forces where he is most likely to break down the defences. We must have self-knowledge, aware of our vulnerable areas, where we are most susceptible to temptation, and put up the battlements through prayer and vigilance.

When we stand in prayer we need to do so with confidence, resisting the approach of the enemy, not being persuaded by his suggestions, nor toying with the temptation or engaging in conversation with the Evil One. That was the great mistake of Eve in the Garden of Eden. She entered into conversation with the Tempter. Almost always a fatal move; the Enemy is too shrewd and a liar from the beginning. He is a coward. If you stand up to him he will flee. But if you cower before him he will ruthlessly seek to destroy you. As Peter says, "Be calm, but vigilant, because your enemy the devil is prowling around like a roaring lion, seeking someone to devour. Stand up to him strong in the faith" (1Pet 5: 8-9).

Teresa of Avila warns her sisters of the devil coming as an "angel of light" offering pleasant consolations in prayer with the intent of leading us away from God. She counsels growing in self-knowledge leading us to humility, which is truth. There are many delusions. Because of little victories we can become smug and over-confident in our capacity not to fall back into our old ways. Instead, we need to move in genuine humility. Often beginners allow themselves to be convinced they are faring so well that they are invincible. On the other hand they can suffer from false humility, feeling unworthy before God and hopeless to advance in holiness. This attitude also is fed by the enemy who delights in feeding us with lies, causing distress and anxiety. There are many deceptions and illusions brought by the devil. "But if one proceeds with humility, strives to know the truth, is subject to a confessor, and communicates with him openly and truthfully… the things the devil intends to cause death will cause life".[67]

Pray at All Times

Prayer is our greatest weapon against the power of temptations that come against us. In the spiritual battle, Paul urges, "Pray at all times, asking for what you need, praying in the Spirit on every possible occasion" (Eph 6:18). Alphonsus Liguori says that we only fall into sin because we have not asked for the Lord's help. He challenges us to reflect on when we have fallen and to see that "the cause of it was that you neglected to beseech God and to seek from him the help needed to battle against the trials with which you were afflicted".[68] We need to pray often for protection, and guard our weak spots, where the defences may be uncertain. In his mercy God will protect us, especially if we cry out in our poverty, and persist in our petition. In our prayer it is particularly effective to give to the Lord our temptations as an offering. In that way we turn them into a means of giving glory to God and a means of grace for us. Then the enemy will not persist, because the reason he tempts us is out of hate for God. If his temptation becomes a means of God being glorified he will flee.

Claiming the Victory

Our prayer to the Father must also claim the victory already won for us in Jesus. After his resurrection, Jesus told Mary Magdalene he was returning to "My father and your father, my God and your God" (Jn 20:17). The Father of Jesus for all eternity is now *our* Father. Jesus has promised, "The will of him who sent me is that I lose nothing of all that he has given me, and I shall raise it up on the last day" (Jn 6:39). And speaking of his followers he said, "The Father who gave them to me is greater than anyone, and no one can steal from the Father" (Jn 10:29). The Enemy comes "to steal to kill and to destroy" (Jn 10:10). But his purpose has been thwarted by what Jesus has accomplished, "I have come that they may have life and to the full" (Jn 10:10). In baptism, when plunged into the water, we go into the tomb with Jesus, and then we rise up with him. The power of his death and resurrection is applied to our lives. As sons and daughters of God, when we pray to the Father in the hour of temptation we are confidently asking the Father of all mercies, who raised Jesus from the dead, to send his Spirit to empower us with resurrection life. We are guaranteed to receive this gift.

There is no inner necessity to sin, even though in the heat of temptation we can feel helpless and overwhelmed. The enemy is the "father of lies" and the "prince of darkness". He will seek to persuade us it is impossible to resist; that there is no way through; the only way is to capitulate. But St Paul reminds us "how infinitely great is the power that he (the Father) has exercised for us believers. This you can tell from the strength of his power at work in Christ when he used it to raise him from the dead" (Eph 1:19-20). In the moment of temptation he wants us to avail of this spiritual power; the power of the Holy Spirit within us which the Father used to raise Christ from the dead! We need to rebuke the lies of Satan and take hold of our birthright in the kingdom of God, as true sons and daughters of the living Father.

Testings in the Church

Some commentators on the Our Father take "temptation" (*peirasmos*) to denote the trial which will come upon humanity with the onset of the final cosmic upheaval, which Jesus predicted will usher in the end of time. The last temptation of our earthly battle will precede the glorious second coming of the Lord. The Book of Revelation gives comforting reassurance to "the church of Philadelphia": "Because you have kept my word of patient endurance, I will keep you from the hour of trial (*peirasmos*) which is coming on the whole world, to try those who dwell upon the earth" (Rev 3:10). The key here is asking for the gift of final perseverance; the grace to be awake when the time comes. "Lo, I am coming like a thief! Blessed is he who is awake" (Rev 16:15). We are praying that when the Lord comes in glory we will have our lamps lit (Mt 25:1-13) and be as the faithful and wise steward of the household who is steadfastly waiting the return of the Master (Lk 12:41-46).

I suggest, with some scholars, that asking not to fall into temptation can be extended also to mean begging for faithfulness in the midst of the trials, persecutions and crises of our present generation. This idea seems to be supported by the Book of Revelation, when the church at Smyrna is told: "Do not be afraid of the sufferings that are coming to you: I tell you the devil is going to send some of you to prison to test you…even if you have to die, keep faithful, and I will give you the crown of life for your prize" (Rev 2: 10). Peter also encourages his people in a similar vein. While they may have to endure all sorts of trials (*peirasmoi*), God has allowed this testing to increase the quality of their faith (1Pet 1:7). He says, "My dear people, you must not think it unaccountable that you should be tested by fire" (1Pet 4:12).

Our testing by fire in any age can take many forms. The Church in our present age is surely being tested by the "tsunami of secularism" in modern culture; a widespread loss of faith, especially in the Western world, which has profoundly affected the Church itself, and threatens to corrode the faith of good people who are not sufficiently grounded in Christ. We have also been shaken to the core by the clergy sexual abuse crisis, exposing an abomination within the Church which will only be overcome by deep repentance and humble reshaping of Church culture to be more aligned to the gospel. In the Our Father we are praying that God's faithful people will not succumb to the temptation to despair and lose faith. We are begging that as Church we will be rebuilt through humble repentance and a vigorous living of the gospel which will reflect the face of Christ today.

DELIVER US FROM EVIL

Jesus' Victory Over Evil

This petition is a deliverance prayer for the whole of humanity, and more specifically for the Church. Evil here is not an abstraction, not a philosophical concept, but an agent of destruction, Satan, the Evil One. Satan is totally opposed to God, but is powerless to directly attack God. Hence he wreaks havoc amongst God's creatures. The manifestations of evil orchestrated by the malevolence of Satan are unfortunately manifold in today's world. Our 24 hour newsfeed keeps spewing out the awful reality of violence, murder, enslavement, torture, human trafficking, drug dealing, economic injustice, starvation, greed, terrorism, war, abortion, euthanasia, and so much more.

Confronted with such dislocation of what it means to be truly human, we do not despair. Our cry for help is full of confidence in the Lord. It is not as if we are inevitably on a sinking ship without hope. To the contrary, our prayer for deliverance arises from conviction of the good news of Jesus Christ. The four gospels are a proclamation that the kingdom of God has come in the person of Jesus Christ and he has decisively, once and for all, overcome the powers of darkness. So this petition dovetails with the earlier cry to the Father, "thy kingdom come".

Kingdom of light over darkness

Jesus' preaching of the kingdom showed his effective power over the demonic forces in the world. When we pray for deliverance from evil we are rejoicing in the redemption already won for us during the ministry of Jesus, and accomplished definitively by his death and resurrection. The gospels present human existence as a battlefield. Humanity will either be dominated by the malevolence of Satan and controlled by his evil spirits, or saved by the incarnate Son of God. Up until the time of Jesus the Evil One had his way. But now a power has come into the world which smashes his game. The Evil One is at work seeking to snatch away the truth of the kingdom being sown into peoples' hearts (Mt 13:19). But Jesus is the stronger one. By his many exorcisms he overcomes the demonic powers. He enters into "the strong man's house", ties him up and burgles his property (Mk 3:27). He says, "If it is by the finger of God I cast out demons then the kingdom of God has come upon you" (Lk 11:20).

At every turn of the page in the gospels Jesus' authority is evident. One time in the synagogue at Capernaum an evil spirit began to manifest while he was preaching. Jesus commanded the spirit to be gone. The people were amazed. This was different than the scribes and Pharisees: "he gives orders even to unclean spirits and they obey him" (Mk 1:27). Often people brought those who were oppressed by an evil spirit to him. The crowds came "to hear him and to be cured of their diseases. People tormented by unclean spirits were also cured, and everyone in the crowd was trying to touch him because power came out of him that cured them all" (Lk 6:18-19).

The classic account of exorcism by Jesus was his confrontation with the Gerasene demoniac (Mk 5:1-20). This tortured man was possessed by evil spirits, his faculties totally out of control, living alone amongst the tombs, and no one could restrain him, even with chains. Night and day he would howl and gash himself with stones. This poor tormented man was delivered by a word from Jesus, commanding the "legion" of demons to come out of him. When the people from the town arrived they were astounded to find the man in his right mind and sitting peacefully with Jesus. The man wanted to stay with Jesus as his disciple. But Jesus sent him to his people to tell them "how much the Lord has done for you". He became the first evangelist for Jesus.

A new authority has come into the world. We are no longer governed by the power of the Evil One. The gospel proclamation of deliverance moves inexorably towards the ultimate victory of the Cross of Jesus. In John, just before Jesus' passion begins, he proclaims, "Now sentence is being passed on this world; now the prince of this world is to be overthrown. And when I am lifted up from the earth, I shall draw all to myself" (Jn 12:32). The "lifting up" of Jesus in Roman crucifixion on Calvary and then through resurrection and ascension brings the absolute defeat of Satan's reign and the ultimate freedom to humanity.

Witnesses of Victory over Evil

While the victory has been won by Christ Jesus, evil powers are still operative in the world. We can sometimes be dismayed by the depths of human depravity and the malevolence of human cruelty and atrocities. Richard Wurmbrand, a Lutheran pastor, relates his experience of human torture during the communist oppression of Romania.[69] A pastor was tortured with red-hot iron pokers and with knives. After being beaten badly, they unleashed large starving rats upon the poor man from which he had to defend himself day and night. The man resisted the efforts of his torturers to force him to betray his fellow Christians. But then they brought in his teenage son and began mercilessly beating the son until the father would provide the information. The man couldn't bear to see what they were doing to his son. It was too much. He cried out for them to stop and he would cooperate. But his son pleaded, "Dad, don't do me the injustice of having a traitor as a parent. Withstand! If they kill me, I will die with the words, 'Jesus and my fatherland'". This enraged the torturers. They beat the boy to death, with his blood splattered over the walls of the cell. He died praising God; victorious in the face of consummate evil.

Wurmbrand gives a blood curling description of the torture he and others had to endure. Their wrists were bound by handcuffs with sharp nails inside[70]. They had to stay totally still to avoid being cut. But in a bitterly cold cell, they couldn't stop involuntarily shivering, and their wrists would be torn and bleeding. Christians were hung upside down on ropes and beaten to pulp. They were placed in icebox "refrigerator cells" with little clothing. Prison doctors watched until they saw symptoms of freezing to death. Then they would give a signal and guards would rush in to take them out and make them warm. Then they would immediately put them back in the icebox to freeze again. The whole procedure would be repeated again and again. They were sometimes forced into wooden boxes with just enough room for the body. The boxes had dozens of nails in the sides with razor sharp points. For endless hours they stood in these boxes trying not to move an inch to avoid the nails piercing the body. Fatigue usually won and they found themselves punctured and bleeding all over. The guards would cry out to them while torturing them, "We are the devil!"

In the face of such unspeakable atrocities we Christians know that Christ is the Victor King. He has won the victory by his loving sacrifice on the Cross. The gospels proclaim the dominion of Satan is ended; the reign of Christ's love has begun. When the first missionary disciples returned, Jesus exclaimed, "I saw Satan fall like lightning from heaven" (Lk 10:18). In the midst of persecution in the early

Church, John, the author of Revelations discloses how war broke out in heaven and the "dragon", Satan, was driven out of heaven. He, "who had deceived all the world was hurled down to earth and his angels hurled down with him". Then John says,

> I heard a voice shout from heaven, 'Victory and power and empire for ever have been won by our God, and all authority for his Christ, now that the persecutor, who accuses the brethren day and night before our God, has been brought down'. (Rev 13:10)

Love conquers

In the worst hell-holes of human atrocity the light of Christ will shine. What Jesus accomplished on the Cross through his loving sacrifice, which was received by the Father in resurrection, has conquered evil. We find the victory of love over hatred. We pray for this victory to be manifest in every deplorable situation. We earnestly pray to the Father: "deliver us from evil". We know through faith that the principalities and powers of evil can be overcome by the spiritual power of God, who is Love.

Wurmbrand tells how during the communist regime an old Romanian priest was thrown into the prison cell occupied by other priests and pastors.[71] This poor man had been brutally tortured. His wounds were so severe he was close to death, and there was no way to assist him. Then later that night, to the surprise of all in the cell, one of the Communist torturers was also thrown into their midst, a much younger man who had been one of the most vicious of their tormentors. Obviously he had fallen foul of the authorities and had been beaten almost to pulp and then dumped in the same cell as his victims.

This young man, who himself was close to death because of the severity of his beating, began to cry out in agony that he was going to die and go to hell because of what he had done, "Help me. I don't want to die. I have committed such terrible crimes". No one in the cell moved. But then, surprisingly, the old dying priest asked two other prisoners to lift him up and take him to the young man. Wurmbrand relates that he saw a miracle of grace which he would never forget. The priest caressed the young man, comforting his murderer. He assured the torturer, "I love you with all my heart". He continued, "If I who am a sinner can love you so much, imagine Christ, who is Love incarnate, how much he loves you". He encouraged the young man to repent of his sins, because Jesus wants to forgive him more than he wanted to be forgiven: "Jesus desires you to be in heaven more than you do".

They all watched and listened in awe as without privacy the young man confessed! The murderer confessed to the one he murdered! And the murdered one gave absolution to his murderer! Then they embraced one another. That night both men died. It was Christmas Eve. Wurmbrand recalls with gratitude: "We were not just celebrating the birth of Christ in Bethlehem, but the birth of Christ in a communist torturer." What a beautiful witness to the victory of love over hatred, of goodness over evil, of forgiveness over vengeance; the victory of the Cross of Jesus, which is our lasting hope.

Contemporary Battle with Evil

While today many are trapped by the evil forces of trafficking in weapons, drugs and human beings, there is a more subtle but deadly enemy in the ideology of self-sufficiency which proclaims God is just a fiction and to believe in him strips you of enjoyment in life. According this mind-set we must be done with God as a useless concept which imprisons us in guilt and powerlessness. But this ideology is blind to the truth; if we lose God we lose ourselves. Without God we have no origin, merely the product of some random evolution, and no ultimate purpose but to live a few years and become extinct. If we succumbed to that world-view the "dragon" would win the day. How we must pray confidently to the Father, "deliver us from evil"! We do not want to be robbed of faith which enables us to see God and encounter Christ, nor do we want to be robbed of our hope which assures us of eternity, a life forever with God. We pray that the human race will be saved from the deception of Satan and the allurement of godless autonomy.

Cyprian, the martyr bishop of Carthage, who endured relentless persecution and ultimately martyrdom, expresses beautifully utmost confidence in victory over adversity, and the protection of faith:

> When we say 'deliver us from evil', then there is nothing further left for us to ask for. Once we have asked for and obtained protection against evil, we are safely sheltered against everything the devil and the world can contrive. What could the world make you fear if you are protected in the world by God himself?[72]

We walk in the assurance of the victory of Christ. But Paul makes it clear that the powers of evil are still roaming the earth. Darkness has been overcome, but the light must be claimed through faith in Christ. We who have given our allegiance to the Christ and his kingdom need to be on guard against the enemy. "For it is not against human enemies that we have to struggle, but against the Sovereignties and Powers who originate the darkness in this world, the spiritual army of evil in the heavens." (Eph 6:11-12) And as John says, "We know that we belong to God but the whole world lies in the power of the Evil

One" (1Jn 5: 19). The battle continues. The devil is like a ferocious dog tied up by a chain. As long as we stay out of the perimeter of his reach we are safe. Foolish is the one who enters into his arena. We must be clothed at all times with the armour of God. Otherwise we will not have the resources to protect ourselves when the worst happens.

For those who have allowed evil spirits to have sway in their personal lives, all is not lost. The Church has been given the gift of deliverance ministry, whereby we can cast out demons in the name of Jesus, no matter what hold they have taken in a person's life.[73] Intercession is crucial during this sort of ministry. We seek first to ask the Holy Spirit to show us what has caused the bondage. We then lead the person to repent and to forgive anyone who has been responsible for wounds inflicted. Then, most importantly, the person needs to renounce any lies or complicity with evil. With the right ground work being done, a simple command by the minister in the name of Jesus for the evil spirits to loosen their hold and be gone suffices to set the person free.

Overcoming Evil within the Church

While Jesus' authority exercised within the Church is certainly an instrument for deliverance from evil, the mystery of iniquity has penetrated the Church itself. While remaining essentially holy, because of the guarantee of the presence of the Holy Spirit, the Church in every age has not been without sinful corruption in its members. Nothing could be more compelling evidence in this age than the sexual abuse of children by priests. Bishop Robert Barron has aptly labelled this scandal as "the devil's masterpiece".[74] Certainly it has struck a devastating blow to the Church and rocked us to our foundations.

The most vulnerable of our own have been unjustly abused leaving their lives devastated; too often remaining shattered people bearing wounds that seem beyond healing. That the abuse has been perpetrated by those ordained to be "men of God" makes it immeasurably more diabolical. The priest is meant to be an icon of Christ, such that his smile is that of Jesus and his word of comfort comes from the mouth of God. When he violates a child or teenager it is experienced as if they were violated by God. As a result the suffering is acute and prolonged; the healing process is not easy. As Church we are struggling to come to grips with how to pastorally care for those offended. We are still in shock and many are traumatised. We have been jolted into keen awareness of the need for a major cultural shift which will provide a child safe environment within the Church's activities, and a place where survivors of abuse can be welcomed and find their place.

The impact on the Church's mission has been catastrophic. This scandal has corroded Catholic credibility so much that our works of evangelisation, catechesis, and outreach to the poor have been seriously crippled. In praying "deliver us from evil" we are interceding for the Church; that we be delivered of this curse of sexual abuse of all kinds; that all the members of the Church, and especially her leaders, would withstand the seduction of the Evil One, and not cooperate with his evil suggestions. To see it as the devil's work does not exonerate those who have been the devil's instruments. Those who have been convicted must face justice, but all of us together share in the shame and guilt for what has happened. Who can take higher ground and claim a superior moral stance? We pray to the Father "deliver us from evil"; that the victory over sin and Satan won through the Cross will be appropriated in the lives of every member of the Church. We have the assurance from Jesus that "the gates of hell will not prevail" over the Church's mission (Mt 16:18). But we must all be shaken out of our torpor, be purified of any compromising attitudes, throw off all worldly behaviour, and cooperate fully with the Lord in his kingdom taking hold on earth through his Church.

Grant Peace in Our Days

In praying "deliver us from evil" we are ultimately asking for God's kingdom to come, for all to be in union with his will, and for the sanctification of his name. Thus, this last petition connects back to the first three. The embolism which we pray in the Mass after the Our Father expresses this:

> Deliver us, Lord, we pray, from every evil,
>
> Graciously grant peace in our days,
>
> That, by the help of your mercy,
>
> We may be always free from sin
>
> And safe from all distress,
>
> As we wait the blessed hope
>
> And coming of our Saviour, Jesus Christ.

We pray for an end to all wars through deeper conversion and peace in our hearts. We pray that we will not sin but will be kept holy by his grace. We pray that all relationships will be restored to harmony, and that we will be delivered from interior conflict, finding a new tranquillity of heart. We beg that all of humanity will be saved from the many distressing situations that afflict us, and we ask for perseverance as we wait for our Saviour to come again.

Unto the Father be Glory

The last petition of this great prayer keeps us sober and watchful, but like all the preceding petitions given to us by Jesus, we must pray as convinced sons and daughters of the everlasting Father. The stance we take when praying the Our Father is as children of God, claiming our full identity as heirs of the kingdom, humbly and confidently lifting our hands to *Abba*, Father. All our trust is in him; we depend on him for everything. Only he is ultimately perfectly trustworthy. As his sons and daughters we have a place in his kingdom. Jesus has made this clear, "Do not be afraid little flock. It has pleased your Father to give you the kingdom" (Lk 12:32).

As I said at the beginning, the whole of this wonderful prayer from the lips of Jesus is about being caught up in the goodness, mercy, kindness and tender heart of our loving Father as his sons and daughters. While praying this prayer we stand in our identity in Christ which we have gained through baptism. We are praying in the Spirit. We are not falling back into the slavery of fear and anxiety, no matter what the circumstances of our personal lives or the state of the Church. Rather we have the Spirit as children of *Abba*, Father, sure of the guarantee given to us in baptism (cf. Rom 8:14-15). Paul reminds us, "Remember it is God himself who assures us all of our standing in Christ, and has anointed us, marking us with his seal and giving us the pledge, the Spirit, that we carry in our hearts" (2Cor 2:21-22). This "pledge" is the guarantee on which our hope is based. The Greek word is *arrabon*, which means a down-payment, much like you might put down an initial payment to purchase a car and say "I will be back". This is what God has done for us in baptism. He has put his seal on us, assuring that we belong to him definitively. He has given us the guarantee of his claim upon us and at the end of our days will return to take us fully into his kingdom.

Every time we pray the Lord's Prayer we are affirming the truth of our recreation as sons and daughters of Abba, Father. We know we are infinitely and unconditionally loved; we are sure of our inestimable worth and dignity, and that nothing can come between us and his love for us. We pray in the Spirit, uttering words that first arose from the heart of Jesus and now we are making our own. We bless God the Father "who in his great mercy has given us a new birth as his sons and daughters, by raising Jesus Christ from the dead, so that we have a sure hope and the promise of an inheritance than can never be spoilt or soiled and never fade away" (1Pet 1:3).

What a privilege it is to pray the Our Father, the very prayer Jesus taught his apostles, and has been faithfully passed down through the centuries until now. This prayer sums up the whole gospel message, and draws into itself all different modes of prayer – praise, worship, contemplation, supplication, intercession, petition, and contrition. Each phrase of the prayer contains endless meanings, some of which I have tried to expound in this volume. In our personal prayer and our liturgies it holds central focus, always being a prayer inclusive of the needs of all people, and when prayed by truly faithful ones is powerful in its effects (James 5:16).

ENDNOTES

1. Teresa of Avila, *The Way of Perfection*, in Collected Works Vol 2 (Washington: ICS Publications, 1980). See an excellent commentary by Aloysius Rego OCD, St Teresa and the Our Father, A Catechism of Prayer, (Oxford: Teresian Press, 2015).

2. Ibid., 27,5

3. Ibid., 28,2

4. Ibid., 28,5

5. Ibid., 28,4

6. St Augustine, *Confessions*, I, (London: Hodder and Stoughton,1983) p.15

7. Ibid., 29,6

8. Ibid., 31,7

9. Ibid., 31,3

10. Ibid., 32,2

11. Bilquis Sheikh, *I Dared to Call him Father*, (Eastbourne: Kingsway Publications, 1979)

12. Steve Biddulph, *Manhood*, Sydney: Ebury Press, 2004.

13. Benedict XVI, *Jesus of Nazareth*, (N.Y.: Doubleday, 2007) p.129

14. *Catechism of the Catholic Church*, 2792

15. Jennifer Moorcroft, *He is My Heaven: The Life of Elizabeth of the Trinity*, (Washington DC:ICS Publications, 2001) p.84

16. Cyprian of Carthage, *On the Lord's Prayer*, 12

17. Benedict XVI, op.cit., p.143

18. St Augustine, *Confessions*, Book 1,1, op.cit.

19. Ibid.

20 Tertullian, *On Prayer*, Ch.3

21 How a Young Chinese girl inspired Archbishop Fulton Sheen to Make a Holy Hour every Day, *Signs and Wonders*, June 9, 2015 on www.sign.org/articles

22 See www.christian today.com/article21christiansslainbyisisto bede-claredmartyrsbycopticchurch/1 March 2015

23 See John O'Brien, *The First Martyrs of North America*, New York: All Saints Press, 1963

24 Pope John Paul II, *Redemptoris Missio*, 18

25 See Pope Francis , Evangelii Gaudium, 24

26 *Gaudium et Spes* (Church in the Modern World) Par.1

27 Pope Francis, *Evangelii Gaudium*, 49

28 Ibid., 46

29 Ibid., 202

30 Ibid., 48

31 Theresa of Avila, *The Way of Perfection*, 32,5 in Collected Works Vol 2 (Washington: ICS Publications, 1980)

32 See Jean-Jacques Antier, *Charles de Foucauld*, (San Francisco: Ignatius Press, 1999)

33 Ibid., p.102

34 *Spiritual Autobiography of Charles de Foucauld*, ed., Jean-Francois Six, (New Jersey: Dimension Books, 1964) p.160

35 Jean-Jacques Antier, op. cit., p.317

36 Ibid., p.340

37 Teresa of Avila, *The Way of Perfection*, 21,2, in Collected Works Vol 2 (Washington: ICS Publications, 1980), p.117

38 Boniface Hanley OFM, *No Strangers to Violence; No Strangers to Love*, (Notre Dame: Ave Maria Press, 1983) p.133

39 Ibid., p.144.

40 St Augustine, Enchiridion 3:11, quoted in *Catechism of the Catholic Church*, 311.

41 Teresa of Avila, *The Way of Perfection*, 32:7

42 John of the Cross, Maxims and Counsels, in *Collected Works* (Washington :ICS Publications, 1979),p.681

43 His story is told in Walter J. Ciszek, S.J., with Daniel L. Flaherty S.J., *With God in Russia*, New York: HarperCollins, 1964. This was followed up by *He Leadeth Me*, San Francisco: Ignatius Press,1973

44 *He Leadeth Me*, p.78

45 Ibid., p.79

46 Ibid., p.89

47 Ibid.

48 Justin Martyr, *Apologia*, 1,67.

49 Cyprian of Carthage, *On the Lord's Prayer*, 19

50 Ibid., 21

51 Ibid., 18

52 St Augustine of Hippo, *Commentary on the Lord's Sermon on the Mount*, trans. D.J.Kavanagh, (Washington: Catholic University of America press, 1951) p.135.

53 St Therese of Lisieux, *Story of a Soul*, (Washington DC: ICS Publications, 1976) p 77

54 Pope Francis, *The Name of God is Mercy*, (London: Pan Macmillan, 2016) p.11

55 Immaculee Ilibagiza, *Left to Tell*, N.Y.: Hayhouse inc., 2006

56 Ibid., p.196

57 Ibid., p.197

58 Ibid., p.204

59 Therese of Lisieux, op.cit., pp 222-223.

60 For more extensive teaching on forgiveness see: Fr Ken Barker MGL, *His Name is Mercy*, Ballan Vic.: Connor Court Publishing, 2010.

61 This story told in Fr Ken Barker, *His Name is Mercy*, op.cit pp 108-111

62 See www.i4give.com

63 See Anne Lim, "Pope's changes to the Lord's Prayer may be valid", www.eternitynews.com.au June 18, 2019

64 *Catechism of the Catholic Church*, 2846

65 Cyprian, *On the Lord's Prayer*, 25

66 This section relies on Ignatius' "Rules for Discernment of Spirits" Nos.13-14 in *The Spiritual Exercises of St Ignatius*, trans. Louis J. Puhl, Chicago: Loyola Press, 1951) pp.145-146

67 Teresa of Avila, *The Way of Perfection* ch.40, Collected Works, op.cit., p.193

68 Alfonsus Liguori, *The Prayer of Petition*, (Ballarat: Majellan Press) p.8

69 Richard Wurmbrand, *Tortured for Christ*, (London: Hodder and Stoughton, 1967) p.29

70 Ibid., p.30-31

71 Pastor Richard Wurmbrand, "An Undying Love", *Again* magazine, September 1987

72 Cyprian, *On the Our Father*, 19

73 See ICCRS Doctrinal Commission, *Deliverance Ministry*, (Rome: ICCRS, 2017)

74 Bishop Robert Barron, *Letter to a Suffering Church*, (Park Ridge: Word on Fire, 2019) Ch.1

www.ingramcontent.com/pod-product-compliance
Lightning Source LLC
Chambersburg PA
CBHW070914160426
43193CB00011B/1451